201 Small-Sided Sports & Games

Small Group and Partner Games for Maximizing Participation, Fitness and Fun in PE!

GUY BAILEY

Educators Press
Vancouver, Washington

Publisher's Cataloging-In-Publication Data
(Prepared by The Donohue Group, Inc.)

Bailey, Guy, 1956-
    201 small-sided sports & games : small group & partner games for maximizing participation, fitness & fun in PE! / Guy Bailey.

    p. : ill. ; cm.

    Includes index.
    ISBN: 978-0-9669727-8-8

    1. Sports for children. 2. Games. 3. Games for two. 4. Physical education for children. 5. Inclusive education. 6. Physical fitness for children. I. Title. II. Title: 201 small-sided sports and games III. Title: Two hundred and one small-sided sports & games

GV709.2 .B35 2013
613.71   2012945719

The author and publisher assume that the reader will teach these games using professional judgment and respect for student safety. In regards to this statement, the author and publisher shall have neither liability nor responsibility in the case of injury to anyone participating in the activities contained within.

EDUCATORS PRESS
14005 NE 8th Street
Vancouver, WA 98684
(360) 597-4355
www.educatorspress.com

Printed in the United States of America

Acknowledgments

Many thanks go out to all of my colleagues in the physical education profession. Because some of the game ideas contained in this resource have been collected from attending workshops and conventions for almost three decades, it's impossible to give specific game credit. However, I have learned so much from you through the sharing of our game ideas and teaching methodology.

Special thanks to my wonderful students at Concord and Sunnyside Elementary Schools who voluntarily played all of these games. I would have had few opportunities to modify and create these game ideas without them. Their exuberance for physical education and game playing was a constant source of inspiration and encouragement.

Thanks also to all of the administrators, staff, and friends that make up the North Clackamas School District in Milwaukie, Oregon. It's been a blessing and an honor to work with all of you. The families in this community are fortunate to have a school board and administrative team that truly value physical education and its many contributions to the overall education of children.

I would also like to acknowledge the many talented professionals that contributed to the design and production of this book. I am particularly indebted to Olga Melnik for her outstanding illustrations. The set-up and play procedures of each game is made easier because of her gift at making games come "alive" for readers.

Finally, an author's family is always owed the greatest amount of gratitude, for they are the ones who truly make the biggest sacrifices. Thank you so much for your constant understanding, encouragement, and support.

"Youngsters are most likely to develop physically active lifestyles if they are provided with physical activity experiences they enjoy and with which they can be successful."

Dr. Russell Pate, President's Council on Physical Fitness & Sports

Preface

The intention of this resource is to provide you with a large selection of small-sided games to get your students genuinely excited about physical education participation while developing specific movement, fitness, and sport skills. These unique games are designed for maximum involvement by all players where everybody is playing all of the time. Each and every one of these skill-based activities has been used successfully with my students and has proven to be fun and enjoyable learning experiences. And, this has happened regardless of class sizes that have been 60 or more!

Unlike many of the traditional, large-group activities, the games in this book have students actively involved 100% of the time playing, learning, and moving. There is no exclusion of students, no standing around, and no waiting for turns. Maximizing participation to enhance learning is patterned after the inclusive style of learning, and it is based on the principle that every child should be included in the learning process 100% of the time. Quite simply, a child cannot benefit from a game or any instructional activity unless he or she is actively involved.

Changing the game rules, boundaries, and strategy of a traditional game is the best way to make any learning experience more inclusive in physical education. And, one of the easiest ways this can be done is to place your students in pairs or small groups. Regardless of class size, you would simply play multiple games simultaneously. For example, in a class of twenty-four students, there would be twelve games being played simultaneously if using one the many partner games described in this book. Now, twenty-four students are actively engaged, learning, and moving 100% of the time. They are also experiencing more skill practicing opportunities, more success, and more fun. Small group and partner activities, with their emphasis on maximum participation, are the core of my physical education program regardless of class size, lesson unit, or play setting.

To help you navigate the book, sections are grouped by a sports theme. Section 1 features games that develop the basketball skills of dribbling, shooting, and passing. Sections 2 through 5 contain small-sided activities that are traditionally categorized as team sports (football, softball, soccer, and floor hockey). Section 6 covers track and field games that are both fun and developmentally appropriate for elementary and middle school students. Section 7 includes scooter games with a sports-related emphasis. Section 8 focuses on gymnastic challenges with an emphasis on upper-body strength development and cooperation. The games in Section 9 ("Sport Duels") are fun one-on-one challenges with a heavy dose of "camouflage" fitness included. Section 10 ("Sports of Sorts") covers miscellaneous sports and games that would be great additions to your lesson as instant starters, ending activities, or as ideas for a station circuit.

Each game provides everything for its successful use, including an introduction with a skill purpose, suggested grade levels, number of players required, equipment needed, and easy-to-understand play instructions. Also included are helpful illustrations to help you visualize the game directions. Before digging into the games, I recommend first reading the section with instructional suggestions and safety guidelines on using small-sided games most effectively in physical education. You will also find advice on the value of competition and cooperation during game playing.

All of us have heard of the often reported studies showing an increase in childhood obesity. It's imperative that children develop healthier lifestyles, which will involve being physically active more often. It's my hope that using these games with your students will meet that need for increased physical activity now—and for a lifetime. It's also my desire that these fun-packed activities will foster a positive attitude toward participation in physical education that is lasting and will leave your students asking to play again and again.

As someone who has taught physical education for more than 30 years and is always looking for new and fun ways to provide quality learning experiences, I trust you'll find *201 Small-Sided Sports & Games* to be a much-used resource and a valuable addition to your professional library. Have fun!

Contents

Section 9: Sport Duels

Section 10: Sports of Sorts!

Using Small-Sided Games in Your Physical Education Program

201 Small-Sided Sports & Games provides the physical educator with a large selection of small-group and partner games to meet the needs of a wide variety of grade levels, interests, and skill proficiencies. The games featured in this book are designed to get students excited about playing, increase their fitness levels, and help them develop specific sport and physical education skills. And, all of these learning experiences call for maximum involvement by all players.

Within each chapter, you will find games placed in a developmentally appropriate arrangement. This lessens your preparation time and makes it quick and easy to find a suitable game. Since student skill proficiencies can vary tremendously within each individual class and grade level, the physical educator should use his or her professional judgment and experience with the students in determining an appropriate game activity. All of the games are suitable for students in elementary and middle school, as well as after-school youth sport settings. To locate a specific game by its title, go to the game index in the back of the book and you will find each activity listed alphabetically.

The explanations for each game are organized in a user-friendly format that shows all of the necessary information you need to know to present the game to your students. This includes:

- **Game Title:** As much as possible, the game title was chosen to give you a descriptive idea of what the activity involves. For example, Football Doubles is a two-on-two football game.
- **Introduction:** Briefly explains the skill objective and play purpose of the activity.
- **Suggested Grade Levels:** Indicates the range of grade levels most appropriate for the activity.
- **Number of Participants:** Tells you how many players are required for the activity.
- **Equipment:** Shows the kind of equipment needed per small-group or partner game. The total amount of equipment per class will be dependent on the number of games being played simultaneously.
- **How to Play:** Explains the set-up procedure and play directions.

The Value of Competition

Competition is inherent to life, regardless of age. For educators to deny this is a refusal of reality and a disservice to their students. Starting at the earliest ages, children will be involved in game playing of some sort at home, school, camps, vacations, etc. And, it continues as we compete for grades, jobs, positions, professional advancement, and so on. In fact, game playing in physical education can offer children valuable opportunities in sportsmanship etiquette and how to handle the emotional aspects of winning and losing that cannot be learned at any other part of the school day. However, there is a difference between good competition and bad competition.

Good competition can bring out the best in a student when it is approached correctly. This is especially true in game playing situations during which the student is encouraged by the teacher to concentrate on his or her personal performance rather than a final score against an opponent. The teaching focus in physical education should always be on using competition to "improve," not to "prove." Good competition does not emphasize winning and losing, nor does it eliminate players, hurt students' feelings, or create hostile environments. The teaching style of an educator, more so than the game, is almost always the deciding factor in whether competition is a positive student experience or not.

Learning the invaluable skill of cooperation is another benefit of game playing and competition. In fact, without cooperation there would be no group games of any size. Following the rules of a game and having the willingness to play with others requires cooperation. Besides cooperation, educators can use game playing and good competition to teach conflict resolution, self-officiating, and game organizational skills for play inside and outside of the gymnasium setting.

Guidelines for Teaching Games

Once you have chosen a game that meets your desired instructional objective, it is time to present it to the students. The following instructional procedures will enhance your presentation of the game while ensuring the safety of your students.

- Avoid situations where children pick the teams. This process is harmful in a number of ways for children, and teachers should implement less threatening methods of group pairing that respect the dignity of each student and promotes positive feelings for physical education.
- Know your students and gain an understanding of their maturity, skill level, height, age, and experience when planning for an activity and matching students.
- Present game rules in a sequential order while being brief and to the point. Try to minimize any wasted instructional time.
- Choose consistent starting and stopping signals.
- Make quick transitions when establishing groups or pairs. Aim for 30 seconds or less.
- Implement creative methods for your students to use when they have issues deciding who goes first, trouble resolving a conflict, and so on. This can be a quick game of Rock, Paper, Scissors, or any other activity that takes minimal time.
- Before play begins, ensure that students have sufficient understanding of the rules.
- Monitor players for fatigue.
- Establish boundaries and identify safety hazards.
- Keep the play area free of obstacles and make sure floors are completely dry.
- Make sure the students are dressed for movement. Require athletic shoes.
- Model the safe use of any special equipment before the start of a game.
- Provide an adequate warm-up, including stretching exercises, prior to the start of play.
- While play is under way, provide positive and constructive feedback with encouragement.

The best bit of advice for teaching any game is to keep it inclusive, involving each student throughout the experience. With greater involvement, students enjoy themselves more and are more receptive to learning. Children love to play, and the use of small-sided games will also provide students the invaluable ingredient of *fun*—which is necessary to stay focused, active, and positive.

Basketball Games

No Rules Basketball

Introduction: This is a great beginning game for children in the primary grades or those with limited basketball experience. This activity introduces many of the offensive and defensive concepts of basketball without the stress of committing a dribbling violation. It's also a nice cardiovascular workout since the game is practically non-stop.

Number of Players: 4–6

Suggested Grade Levels: K–3rd grades

Equipment: 1 basketball, 1 hoop, player identification vests

How to Play: Form two equal teams of two or three players. The game can be played on either a regulation court or a half-court. Designate one team to start on offense.

Since there is no jump ball to start the game, the designated offensive team passes the ball inbounds from the backcourt area. The players are allowed to dribble, walk, or run with the ball and can take as long as needed to move the ball toward the basket. No traveling or double dribble violations are called. As a consequence, the better-skilled players can dribble and the less-skilled players can choose how to move with the ball without the anxiety of penalties. Defensive players are not allowed to foul. Violations such as fouls or rough play result in a team gaining possession with a throw-in.

A successful shot counts as two points. After each score, the non-scoring team passes the ball in from the end line behind the basket.

No Swipe Basketball

Introduction: This basketball game allows the less experienced player the opportunity to handle the ball without defensive pressure. It's also a good choice for children who want to enjoy playing basketball without the need of an official to call fouls.

Number of Players: 4–6

Suggested Grade Levels: 3rd–8th grades

Equipment: 1 basketball, 1 hoop, player identification vests

How to Play: Form two equal teams of two or three players. The game can be played on either a regulation court or a half-court. Designate one team to start on offense.

Since there is no jump ball to start the game, the designated offensive team passes the ball inbounds from the backcourt area. Regular dribbling and basketball rules are used except defensive players cannot steal the ball from the dribbler. However, if the dribbler losses control of the dribble, passes the ball, or takes a shot, then any opposing player can intercept or gain control of the ball. Violations such as a foul or rough play result in a team gaining possession with a throw-in.

A successful shot counts as two points. After each score, the non-scoring team passes the ball in from the end line behind the basket.

No Dribble Basketball

Introduction: This activity introduces young players to the game of basketball without the stress of dribbling (one of the more difficult aspects of basketball). With the exception of dribbling, all of the major skills of playing basketball are being developed. It's also a great activity at getting every player actively involved since the ball can only be advanced down the court by passing.

Number of Players: 4–6

Suggested Grade Levels: 3rd–8th grades

Equipment: 1 basketball, 1 hoop, player identification vests

How to Play: Form two equal teams of two or three players. The game can be played on either a regulation court or a half-court. Designate one team to start on offense.

Since there is no jump ball to start the game, the designated offensive team passes the ball inbounds from the backcourt area. Regular basketball rules are used except offensive players cannot dribble. However, if the offensive player losses control of the ball, passes the ball, or takes a shot, then any opposing player can intercept or gain control of the ball. Violations such as fouls, dribbling, or rough play results in a team gaining possession with a throw-in.

A successful shot counts as two points. After each score, the non-scoring team passes the ball in from the end line behind the basket.

Basketball Duel

Introduction: Basketball Duel maximizes ball handling opportunities and requires tremendous hustle. With the exception of passing, all of the major skills of playing basketball are being developed.

Number of Players: 2

Suggested Grade Levels: 4th–8th grades

Equipment: 1 basketball, 1 hoop, player identification vests

How to Play: Assign one player to play another. The game can be played on either a regulation court or a half-court. Designate one player to start on offense.

Since there is no jump ball to start the game, the designated offensive player dribbles the ball inbounds from the backcourt area. Regular basketball rules are used except the offensive player cannot pass. An offensive player who stops dribbling must shoot from that spot. Violations such as fouls, traveling, or rough play results in the other player gaining possession with a dribble-in from the nearest boundary line.

A successful shot counts as two points. After each score, the non-scoring player dribbles the ball in from the end line behind the basket or the boundary line on top if playing half-court.

Basketball Doubles

Introduction: As the name implies, Basketball Doubles is two-on-two basketball. This game is a natural progression of Basketball Duel (one-on-one basketball) and maximizes ball handling opportunities. All of the major skills of playing basketball are developed.

Number of Players: 4

Suggested Grade Levels: 4th–8th grades

Equipment: 1 basketball, 1 hoop, player identification vests

How to Play: This game requires four players. Two players start on offense with the ball while the other two players are on defense. The game can be played on either a regulation court or a half-court.

Since there is no jump ball to start the game, the designated offensive team passes the ball inbounds from the backcourt area. Regular basketball rules are used except there are no free throw shots after a foul violation. Violations such as fouls, traveling, or rough play results in the other team gaining possession with a dribble-in from the nearest boundary line.

A successful shot counts as two points. After each score, the non-scoring team passes the ball in from the end line behind the basket or the boundary line on top if playing half-court.

Half-Court Challenge

Introduction: This game is a favorite on driveways and playgrounds around the world. Its many advantages are that it doesn't require many players, has fewer rules than regular basketball, and is played with just one hoop. All of the major skills of playing basketball are being developed.

Number of Players: 4–6

Suggested Grade Levels: 4th–8th grades

Equipment: 1 basketball, 1 hoop, player identification vests

How to Play: Although any number of players can participate, this game is best played with two equal teams of two-three players each. One team starts on offense with the ball with the other team on defense. The game is played on a half-court, with the mid-court line used as a boundary. Both teams will be shooting at the same hoop.

Since there is no jump ball to start the game, the designated offensive team passes the ball inbounds from the backcourt area. Regular basketball rules are used except there are no free throw shots after a foul violation. Violations such as fouls, traveling, or rough play results in the other team gaining possession with a dribble-in from the nearest boundary line. If a ball changes possession, the team gaining possession must take the ball past the extended free throw line before attempting a shot.

A successful shot counts as two points. After each score, the non-scoring team passes the ball in from the boundary line on top of the half-court.

In & Out Basketball

Introduction: This three-team game is played exactly like Half-Court Challenge (page 19), except after each score, the non-scoring team exits the court and a waiting team enters and starts on offense. All of the major skills of basketball are developed in this activity.

Number of Players: 6

Suggested Grade Levels: 4th–8th grades

Equipment: 1 basketball, 1 hoop, player identification vests

How to Play: Although any number of players can participate, this game is best played with three equal and small-sided teams (for example, two-on-two-on-two). One team starts on offense with the ball with one team on defense and a third team standing off to the sideline. The game is played on a half-court, with the mid-court line used as a boundary and both teams shooting at the same hoop.

Since there is no jump ball to start the game, the designated offensive team passes the ball inbounds from the backcourt area. Regular basketball rules are used except there are no free throw shots after a foul violation. Violations such as fouls, traveling, or rough play results in the other team gaining possession with a dribble-in from the nearest boundary line. If a ball changes possession, the team gaining possession must take the ball past the extended free throw line before attempting a shot.

A successful shot counts as two points. After each score, the non-scoring team exchanges place with the third team that has been waiting off to the side. The new offensive team passes the ball in from the boundary line on top of the half-court. Play continues with this rotation of teams throughout the game.

Basketball Triplets

Introduction: This game is essentially one-on-one-on-one basketball with each player being a "team." It's a terrific activity for developing many of the major skills of basketball in a fun and active setting.

Number of Players: 3

Suggested Grade Levels: 4th–8th grades

Equipment: 1 basketball, 1 hoop, player identification vests

How to Play: This game requires three players. One player starts on offense with the ball while the other two players are on defense. The game can be played on either a regulation court or a half-court.

The designated offensive player starts the game by dribbling the ball inbounds from the backcourt area. The offensive player attempts to move the ball into position to shoot and make a basket while the two defensive players work together to stop the offensive player from scoring. A defensive player who steals the ball or rebounds a missed shot becomes the new offensive player, and the previous offensive player now becomes one of the defensive players. A dribbling violation on the offensive player results in a jump ball between the two defensive players (the offensive player tosses the jump ball). Regular basketball rules are used except there are no free throw shots after a foul violation. Instead, the fouled player dribbles the ball inbounds from the nearest boundary line.

A successful shot counts as two points. After each score, the non-scoring team passes the ball in from the end line behind the basket or the boundary line on top if playing half-court.

Horse

Introduction: Horse is a popular basketball shooting contest played by children at recess, driveways and playgrounds across the country. A wide variety of shots can be practiced in this classic game.

Number of Players: 2–3

Suggested Grade Levels: 3rd–8th grades

Equipment: 1 basketball, 1 hoop

How To Play: Although any number of players can participate, this game is best played with small-sided groups (two or three players) assigned to each available hoop. Before beginning, players establish a shooting order.

To start, the first player tries to shoot a basket from anywhere on the court. If successful, the next player in line must also make a basket from the exact same spot using the exact type of shot. If the second player or any later player fails to make the shot, each is assigned the letter H. If a player makes the shot, no letter is assigned. After everyone has had a turn at shooting, the first player regains the ball and can take a shot from anywhere. Again, if successful, the other players must imitate it. If the initial shooter misses a shot, the second player then has the opportunity to take a shot from anywhere on the court. The objective is to make a shot and hope that the next player misses, causing the letters H-O-R-S-E to be spelled against them. A player is out of the game once he or she has all of the letters. Play continues until only one player remains.

It's recommended that an alternative practice shooting area be set aside for any players who have to exit before the others are finished. Alternatively, early exciters can also form new groups and begin a new game at another hoop. This way, all players are actively practicing their shooting skills.

Around the World

Introduction: This classic shooting game has long been a favorite with children and adults alike. Shooting skills from a variety of distances and locations are developed in this easy-to-play activity.

Number of Players: 2–3

Suggested Grade Levels: 3rd–8th grades

Equipment: 1 basketball, 1 hoop

How to Play: Although any number of players can participate, this game is best played with two or three players assigned to each available hoop. Designate eight shooting spots around the goal as shown in the illustration below.

Before beginning, players establish a shooting order. To start, the first player attempts two shots from spot #1. If successful, he or she advances to spot #2. If unsuccessful, the next player in line shoots from spot #1. As long as a player is successful with one of the two shots, he or she keeps advancing to the next spot. The objective is to be the first player to make baskets from each of the eight spots, and back again.

After missing two shots, players always begin again at spot #1 on their next turn. However, after missing the first shot, allow players the option of taking a second shot attempt or forgoing it so that they continue their next turn from the spot they previously stopped.

Bump

Introduction: This competitive shooting game allows players the opportunity to practice shooting skills while reinforcing the basketball concepts of hustling and concentration.

Number of Players: 3

Suggested Grade Levels: 4th–8th grades

Equipment: 2 basketballs, 1 hoop

How to Play: This game is best played with three participants assigned to each available hoop. Before beginning, players establish a shooting order and stand in a single file formation behind the free throw line. The first two players in line each begin with a basketball.

To start, the first player attempts a shot from the free throw line. If the shot is good, the player retrieves the ball, passes it to the next player in line without a basketball, and goes to the end of the line. If the first player misses the first shot, he or she retrieves the ball and keeps trying to make a basket from anywhere on the court. Meanwhile, the second player in line shoots from the free throw line immediately after the first player's missed shot. If the shot goes in before the first player makes a follow-up basket, the first player is out. The objective is always to "bump" the previous player out of the game by making a basket before he or she does. Play continues in this fashion until only one player remains.

To maximize participation, consider playing a "no out" version where players are awarded one point for bumping out another player, but the bumped player remains in the game. The objective is to earn more points than the others.

Basketball Frenzy

Introduction: This one-minute shootout allows players the opportunity to practice shooting skills from a variety of distances and requires great hustle at rebounding.

Number of Players: 2

Suggested Grade Levels: 4th–8th grades

Equipment: 1 basketball, 1 hoop, stopwatch (if needed)

How to Play: This game is played with two participants assigned to each available hoop. Select one player to start with the basketball.

Time the activity for one minute, with the first player shooting from anywhere on the court. The second player quickly rebounds and shoots from the spot of his or her choice. A basket counts as two points. The two players alternate shot attempts as quickly as possible in this fashion until one minute is up. To reinforce shooting from a variety of areas, require players to shoot from a different spot each time. The objective is to end the contest with the most points.

A great variation, if playing with two pairs of players at the same hoop, is to have each of the two players (in a pair) add their point total together and try to end up with more points than the other "team" of two players.

Basketball Golf

Introduction: This unique shooting game allows players the opportunity to practice shooting skills from a variety of distances and spots while using the scorekeeping concepts of golf.

Number of Players: 2–3

Suggested Grade Levels: 4th–8th grades

Equipment: 1 basketball, 1 hoop, 9 poly spots (or substitute hula hoops)

How to Play: This game is best played with two or three participants assigned to each available hoop.

Design a "golf course" around a basket by placing nine poly spots (or substitute hula hoops) in various locations. Create a wide variety of shots to be used by having players shoot from the corner, free throw line, and so forth. Since each poly spot represents a golf hole, assign a number to each spot. Players establish a shooting order. If needed, hand each player a scorecard and pencil.

The game begins with each player, in turn, shooting from Hole #1 until he or she makes the shot. The number of times needed to make the shot is recorded. When everyone is finished, the group moves to Hole #2, and each player continues to make a basket in as few attempts possible. Players keep score as they would if playing golf, with each shot counting as a "stroke." The objective is to have the lowest score by finishing the course with the fewest shot attempts.

Twenty-One

Introduction: This is another popular shooting game that allows players the opportunity to practice foul-shooting and layup techniques while engaging in fun competition with others. The risk of going over 21 points and having to start all over again adds to the excitement of this activity.

Number of Players: 2–3

Equipment: 1 basketball, 1 hoop

Suggested Grade Levels: 3rd–8th grades

How To Play: Although any number of players can participate, this game is best played with small-sided groups (two or three players) assigned to each available hoop.

Before beginning, players establish a shooting order and stand in a single file formation behind the free throw line. The first player in line begins with the ball. To start, the first player attempts a shot from the free throw line and a follow-up shot from either the spot of the rebound or a lay-up attempt. The free throw shot, if made, counts as two points and the follow-up shot counts as one point. After both shot attempts, the ball is handed to the next player in line who does the same. The objective is to be the first player to reach exactly 21 points. Since a score over 21 points results in a player having to start all over again, a player needs to be careful which shots he or she makes (or deliberately misses) toward the end of play.

Basketball Juggling

Introduction: This small-group basketball activity develops passing and catching skills. The excitement of "juggling" several basketballs at one time will make it a favorite among your students.

Number of Players: 5

Suggested Grade Levels: 4th–8th grades

Equipment: 2–4 basketballs

How to Play: The players start in a circular formation as shown in the illustration. Select one player (player #1) to start with the basketball, with several additional basketballs placed on the floor behind the player with the ball.

On a starting signal, the player with the basketball (#1) passes to player #2. Player #2 passes to player #3, and so on. The "star" pattern continues until the ball gets back to where it started. Once the group has mastered the pattern, have player #1 add a second ball immediately after passing the first ball. Each ball must follow the same pattern. The objective is to keep adding basketballs to see how many a group can keep in play (up to four balls is the recommended maximum).

Caution the players to stay alert, avoid passing a ball toward a teammate's head, and to keep their eyes focused on the player passing the ball toward them.

Basketball Bull

Introduction: This "keep-a-away" type game develops the basketball skills of passing, catching, and ball stealing.

Number of Players: 4–6

Suggested Grade Levels: 4th–8th grades

Equipment: 1 basketball, 1 hoop

How to Play: Basketball Bull is best played with 4-6 participants. With the exception of the Bull, the players start in a circular formation as shown in the illustration. Select one player to start with the basketball, and one player to start in the middle of the circle as the Bull.

On a starting signal, the players standing around the circle pass the basketball back and forth while the Bull attempts to touch or intercept a pass by quickly charging after it. If successful, the Bull trades places with the player who last touched the ball. The objective for the circle players is to last as long as possible without becoming a Bull.

To encourage accurate passing, require a circle player to become the next Bull if he or she makes an errant pass that exits the circle.

Basketball Duck & Goose

Introduction: This exciting basketball game is played with only two players and contains the tag element used in the traditional game of "Duck, Duck, Goose." Dribbling, passing, and catching are the main skills utilized.

Number of Players: 2

Suggested Grade Levels: 4th–8th grades

Equipment: 1 basketball, 2 cones (or tape) to mark off lines

How to Play: Each player stands facing a partner about 6 feet apart. A "safety" line is marked off about 20-30 feet behind each player. One player is designated to start with the basketball.

The player with the basketball begins the game by saying "Duck" and passing the ball to the other player. The other player receives the pass, repeats the same word ("Duck") and passes the ball back. At any time, one of the players can yell out "Goose" after passing the ball. At this time, the player receiving the pass (the Goose) would dribble and chase the other player toward his or her safety line attempting to make a tag with the non-dribbling hand. The objective for the fleeing player is to make it to the safety line without getting tagged by the Goose. After each turn, the two players always return to the middle and repeat the passing and chanting of "Duck, Duck, Goose."

Basketball Bandit

Introduction: Basketball Bandit is a chasing and fleeing game that enhances the skills of dribbling, ball control, and stealing.

Number of Players: 2

Suggested Grade Levels: 3rd–8th grades

Equipment: 1 basketball

How to Play: This one-on-one game is best played on a half basketball court, or anywhere a good dribbling surface exists. If several games are being played simultaneously, it might be best to mark off a smaller designated play area for each pair of players. Assign one player to start with the basketball as the dribbler, and the other player without a basketball begins as the ball stealer (or Bandit).

On a starting signal, the Bandit chases the dribbler and attempts to steal his or her basketball. A dribbler who loses the basketball becomes the new Bandit. The objective for the dribbler is to last as long as possible without becoming a Bandit. The Bandit cannot touch or foul the dribbler when attempting a steal. Dribblers must dribble continuously throughout the game using legal dribbling techniques. To encourage correct dribbling techniques, have the two player exchange roles if a dribbling violation occurs.

The Moving Star

Introduction: The Moving Star emphasizes the skills of passing and catching, and is a natural progression of Basketball Juggling (page 28). It is also a great cardiovascular workout.

Number of Players: 5

Suggested Grade Levels: 4th–8th grades

Equipment: 1 basketball

How to Play: The Moving Star is played with five participants. The players start in a circular formation as shown in the illustration. Select one player (player #1) to start with the basketball.

Before play, have the players practice passing the ball in a "star" pattern as shown in the illustration. The player with the basketball (#1) passes to player #2. Player #2 passes to player #3, and so on. The "star" pattern continues until the ball gets back to where it started. Once the group has mastered the pattern, add the "moving" part. After player #1 passes the ball, he or she immediately runs counterclockwise around the outside of the circle to his/her original spot. Each subsequent player receiving a pass immediately runs in the same fashion (after passing the ball first). The objective is for each runner to arrive back to his/her original spot before the ball gets there. Have the players use different types of passes (chest, bounce, etc.) with each round.

Caution the players to stay alert, avoid passing a ball toward a teammate's head, and to keep their eyes focused on the player passing the ball toward them.

Basketball Hounds

Introduction: This "give & go" game develops the basketball skills of passing, catching, and pivoting. This combination of using basketball skills with the fun of playing tag has proven to be a student favorite.

Number of Players: 3–5

Suggested Grade Levels: 3rd–8th grades

Equipment: 1 basketball, marking tape or cones

How to Play: Basketball Hounds is best played with 3-5 participants. With the exception of one player (the Fox), the players start in a scattered formation in a marked off area about 10' x 10' in size. Select one player to start with the basketball, and one player to start in the middle of the box as the Fox. The player with the basketball and all other players beside the Fox are called "Hounds."

On a starting signal, the players (Hounds) pass the basketball back and forth attempting to tag the Fox with the basketball held in two hands. The Hound with the ball cannot run or walk — a pivot is the only movement allowed. Hounds without the ball should move into a position close enough to the Fox to receive a pass. The key is for the Hounds to pass quickly and move as soon they pass the ball (the "give and go" concept). If a successful tag is made, the Fox trades places with the Hound who tagged him or her. The objective for the Fox is to last as long as possible without becoming a Hound.

Dribble Gotcha

Introduction: This fantastic dribbling game reinforces the importance of dribbling with the eyes up, while also improving ball handling and stealing skills. Because both players are dribbling and stealing at the same time, the constant activity also improves cardiovascular endurance.

Number of Players: 2

Suggested Grade Levels: 4th–8th grades

Equipment: 2 basketballs (1 for each player)

How to Play: This one-on-one game is best in a marked off area of about 10' x 10' in size. Both players begin with a basketball.

On a starting signal, the players dribble and attempt to knock away the opponent's basketball using their free hand. At the same, each player is defending against having the opponent knock his or her own ball away! A player yells out "Gotcha" each time he or she successfully knocks away the opponent's basketball. A player who loses the ball quickly retrieves it and rejoins the game. Players must dribble continuously throughout the game using only legal dribbling techniques. Rough play and fouling is not allowed. The objective of the game is to have more "Gotchas" than the opponent.

Dribble Tag

Introduction: This simple and fun game develops the basketball skills of dribbling, ball control, and ball stealing. The chasing and fleeing nature of the game also improves cardiovascular endurance.

Number of Players: 2

Suggested Grade Levels: 4th–8th grades

Equipment: 1 basketball, 1 set of football flags for each player

How to Play: This one-on-one game is best on a half basketball court or a smaller marked-off area if several groups are playing simultaneously. Both players wear football flags for pulling. Select one player to start with the basketball as the dribbler, and one player to start without the basketball as the chaser.

On a starting signal, the player with the basketball starts dribbling while the other player gives chase attempting to pull one of the dribbler's flags. If successful, the two players trades places with the former dribbler now doing the chasing. The objective for the dribbler is to last as long as possible without having a flag pulled. Dribblers must dribble continuously using legal dribbling techniques, and chasers are not allowed to touch or foul the dribbler.

Dribble Knock Down

Introduction: This challenging and fun game reinforces the importance of dribbling with the eyes up. Because both players are dribbling and knocking down a cone at the same time, the non-stop action will improve cardiovascular endurance.

Number of Players: 2

Suggested Grade Levels: 4th–8th grades

Equipment: 2 basketballs (1 for each player), 1 cone

How to Play: This one-on-one game is played with a cone placed between the two players who are facing each other a few feet apart. Both players begin with a basketball. Assign one player as the "Knock it Downer," and the other player as the "Set it Upper."

The players begin by dribbling with the "Knock it Downer" player attempting to knock the cone over with his or her free hand, with the "Set it Upper" player returning the cone to its upright position with the free hand. A player who loses the ball quickly retrieves it and rejoins the game. Players must dribble continuously throughout the game using only legal dribbling techniques. The objective of the game is have more "knock downs" or "set ups" than the opponent. After a pre-determined time, have the players change roles and play again.

Dribbling Stare Down

Introduction: This partner game reinforces the importance of dribbling with the eyes up while, at the same time, having a fun "staring contest."

Number of Players: 2

Suggested Grade Levels: 4th–8th grades

Equipment: 2 basketballs (1 for each player)

How to Play: This one-on-one game can be played anywhere that has a hard surface for dribbling. Both players begin with a basketball.

The players begin by facing their partner and looking into each other's eyes while dribbling in place. A student scores a point every time their partner blinks, looks away, or loses control of the ball.

Variations: If playing with a large group of participants, have the players find new partners after each stare down. Older players might also enjoy this activity by dribbling with two basketballs at the same time while staring.

Dribble Fencing

Introduction: This dribbling duel reinforces the importance of dribbling with the eyes up, while also improving ball handling skills. Because of the non-stop movement, this game also improves cardio-vascular endurance.

Number of Players: 2

Suggested Grade Levels: 4th–8th grades

Equipment: 2 basketballs and 2 pool noodles (1 for each player)

How to Play: This one-on-one game is best in a marked off area of about 10' x 10' in size. Both players begin with a basketball and a foam pool noodle. On a starting signal, the players dribble and attempt to knock away their opponent's basketball using the pool noodle (the "sword") held in their free hand. At the same, each player is defending against having the opponent knock his or her own ball away! A player receives one point each time he or she successfully knocks away the opponent's basketball with their sword. A player who loses the ball quickly retrieves it and rejoins the game. Players must dribble continuously throughout the game using only legal dribbling techniques. Rough play and fouling is not allowed. The objective of the game is to have more points than their opponent.

Variation: Have the two players play a "tag" type of game during which one player begins with the ball (but no pool noodle) and one player with a pool noodle (but no basketball). The "It" with the sword chases the player dribbling and attempts to tag the player by touching the basketball with the sword. If successful, the players trade places.

Dribble Dancing

Introduction: This fun activity develops a variety of dribbling skills—dominant hand, non-dominant, alternating—while working cooperatively with a partner. Creative and critical thinking skills are also utilized in this activity.

Number of Players: 2

Suggested Grade Levels: 4th–8th grades

Equipment: 2 basketballs (1 for each player)

How to Play: This partner game can be played anywhere that has a hard surface for dribbling. Both players begin with a basketball, and both should have similar dribbling skill levels.

The players begin by creating a dribbling routine using a variety of dribbling skills. Each pair can be as creative as needed to come up their own unique "dance." For example, using a square dance format, the students can dribble around each other with a "do-sa-do" movement, hold right hands and perform an "allemande" while dribbling with the left hand, perform a partner "swing" with each student locking inside arms and walking in a circular direction while dribbling with the outside hands, and so forth.

Variations: Have the players add passing and/or fancy dribbling challenges to their routine. Also, if multiple participants are available, consider forming a square dance group of 4-8 players and have them perform a basketball square dance as a group.

Dribbling Math Duel

Introduction: This unique game reinforces the importance of dribbling a basketball with the eyes up. It also integrates math practice with physical education.

Number of Players: 2

Suggested Grade Levels: 4th–8th grades

Equipment: 2 basketballs (1 for each player)

How to Play: This partner game can be played on any hard surface. Both players begin with a basketball.

The two players begin by facing each other and dribbling in place with one hand. At any time, the players count out loud to three and then flash a certain number of fingers with their free hand. One point is awarded to the first player to correctly say the sum of the numbers shown. The players do not stop dribbling when the numbers are flashed and added — dribbling is constant.

Variations: Depending on their math abilities and grade level, have the students perform the activity by subtracting or multiplying the flashed numbers. If playing with multiple participants, have the players dribble freely around and get a new partner after each math encounter.

Mouse Tail Dribble

Introduction: This student favorite develops dribbling skills, and the non-stop nature of this activity also improves cardiovascular endurance.

Number of Players: 2

Suggested Grade Levels: 3rd–8th grades

Equipment: 2 basketballs (1 for each player), 1 jump rope

How to Play: This one-on-one game is best on a basketball court or any place that has a hard surface for dribbling. Both players each have a basketball. Select one player (the Mouse) to start with a 6' jump rope held lightly with two fingers, and one player to start as the chaser (the Cat).

On a starting signal, the Cat pursues the Mouse who is dribbling with one hand and holding a rope with the other hand. The Cat dribbles with one hand while chasing and attempts to step on the rope (causing it to pull free from the Mouse's hand). If successful, the two players trade places. The objective for the Mouse is to last as long as possible without having his or her rope stepped on and pulled. Both players must dribble continuously using legal dribbling techniques, and chasers are not allowed to touch or foul the dribbler.

Floor Hockey Games

Floor Hockey Duel

Introduction: This one-on-one game maximizes stick handling opportunities and requires tremendous hustle. With the exception of passing, all of the major skills of playing floor hockey are being developed.

Number of Players: 2

Suggested Grade Levels: 3rd–8th grades

Equipment: 1 hockey stick for each player, 1 puck, 2 cones

How to Play: The play area consists of two cones placed approximately 15-20 feet apart. There are no boundary lines. The two players start in the middle of the two cones, with each facing the cone that they will attempt to hit with the puck.

The game begins with a "face-off" (a series of three taps with the sticks before hitting the puck) in the middle of the two cones. The objective is to control the puck and drive toward the opponent's cone in order to shoot and hit it for a score. If successful, one point is scored and the puck is placed back in the middle for another face-off. A player may attempt to steal the puck at any time to become the offensive player. Since there are boundary lines, players can shoot and hit an opponent's cone from any angle.

No player can touch the puck with his or her hands, and no physical contact (including high-sticking) is allowed. A violation results in the other player gaining possession at the spot of the infraction.

Floor Hockey Doubles

Introduction: This two-on-two activity is a natural progression of Floor Hockey Duel (one-on-one floor hockey) and maximizes stick handling opportunities. All of the major skills of playing floor hockey are being developed along with lots of healthy movement.

Number of Players: 4

Suggested Grade Levels: 3rd–8th grades

Equipment: 1 hockey stick for each player, 1 puck, 2 cones

How to Play: The play area consists of two cones placed about 20 feet apart. There are no boundary lines. Form two teams of two players each. There are no designated positions, although playing the goalie position should be limited (instead, passing and offensive teamwork should be encouraged).

This game is played much like Floor Hockey Duel (page 44) except now there are two players on each team and the skill of passing is utilized. Two opposing players start with a face-off in the middle of the play area. The objective is to control the puck and drive toward the opponent's cone in order to shoot and hit the cone for a score. If successful, one point is scored and the puck is brought back to the middle for another face-off. Defensive players may attempt to steal the puck at any time to gain possession. Since there are no boundary lines, players can shoot and hit an opponent's cone from any angle.

Rough play, including high-sticking, is not allowed. A violation results in the other team gaining possession of the puck at the spot of the infraction.

Mini Floor Hockey

Introduction: This three-on-three activity is a natural progression of Floor Hockey Duel (one-on-one hockey) and Floor Hockey Doubles (two-on-two hockey). It maximizes stick handling opportunities and enhances all of the major skills of playing floor hockey.

Number of Players: 6

Suggested Grade Levels: 4th–8th grades

Equipment: 1 hockey stick for each player, 1 puck, 4 cones

How to Play: The play area consists of two goals about 20-30 feet apart. For goals, place two cones about 5 feet apart. There are no boundary lines. Form two teams of three players each. Designate two forwards and one goalie on each team.

This game is played much like Floor Hockey Doubles (page 45) except now there are three players on each team and the position of goalie is introduced. Two opposing players start with a face-off in the middle of the play area. The objective is to control the puck and drive toward the opponent's goal in order to shoot and hit the puck through the two cones for a score. If successful, one point is scored and the puck is brought back to the middle for another face-off. Defensive players may attempt to steal the puck at any time to gain possession. Since there are no boundary lines, players can shoot and score from any angle (including backwards through the two cones). Have teammates rotate positions throughout the game.

Floor Hockey Twins

Introduction: The players on each team form "three-legged" teams, and compete against each other in a game that offers lots of cooperative movement, fun, and laughter.

Number of Players: 4

Suggested Grade Levels: 4th–8th grades

Equipment: 1 hockey stick for each pair of players, 1 puck, football flag belts (for strapping the legs together), 2 cones

How to Play: The play area consists of two cones placed about 20 feet apart. There are no boundary lines. Form two teams of two players each. Using the football belts, the two teammates strap their inside legs together to form a "three-legged team." There are no designated positions.

This game is played much like Floor Hockey Doubles (page 45) except now the two players on each team form a three-legged team. The "twins" start with a face-off in the middle of the play area. The objective is to control the puck and drive toward the opponent's cone in order to shoot and hit the cone for a score. If successful, one point is scored and the puck is brought back to the middle for another face-off. Defensive players may attempt to steal the puck at any time to gain possession. Since there are no boundary lines, players can shoot and hit an opponent's cone from any angle.

Variation: Consider playing a three-on-three version of this game with one individual goalie on each team to go along with the two twins. The play area would consist of having two cones placed about 5 feet apart at each end for goals.

Hockey Pirates

Introduction: Hockey Pirates is a highly engaged and active game that enhances the hockey skills of puck control and stealing.

Number of Players: 4

Suggested Grade Levels: 3rd–8th grades

Equipment: 1 hockey stick for each player, 4 pucks, marking tape

How to Play: With the marking tape, make 5 circles (about 4 feet in diameter) in a formation as shown in the illustration below. Place all four pucks in the middle circle. Each player, with hockey stick in hand, stands inside one of the four corner circles.

On a starting signal, all four players move toward the center circle, take one puck with their hockey stick, and move it back toward their circle (placing it inside the circle). At this point, each player attempts to steal a puck from another circle while guarding against his/her own puck being stolen. The objective is to be the first player to have two pucks inside his/her circle.

Variation: For three player groups, set up a triangular shaped play area with one circle in the middle. The same rules as described above would still apply.

Hockey Bandit

Introduction: Hockey Bandit is a chasing and fleeing game that enhances the floor hockey skills of puck control and stealing. It is also a very active game which builds cardiovascular fitness.

Number of Players: 2

Suggested Grade Levels: 3rd–8th grades

Equipment: 1 hockey stick for each player, 1 puck

How to Play: This one-on-one game is best played on a half basketball court, or anywhere a good hockey playing surface exists. If several games are being played simultaneously, it might be best to mark off a smaller designated play area for each pair of players. Assign one player to start with the puck, and the other player begins without the puck as the puck stealer (or Bandit).

On a starting signal, the Bandit chases the player with the puck and attempts to steal it away. A player who loses the puck becomes the new Bandit. The objective for the player with the puck is to last as long as possible without becoming a Bandit. The Bandit cannot touch the other player while attempting a steal. Players with the puck must move continuously throughout the game using legal puck control techniques. To encourage correct puck control techniques, have the two player exchange roles if high-sticking or any other violation occurs.

Hockey Croquet

Introduction: This dual-sport game develops hockey striking skills while using the strategies of playing croquet.

Number of Players: 2-4

Suggested Grade Levels: 3rd–8th grades

Equipment: 1 hockey stick for each player, 1 puck, 4 cones

How to Play: Assign two or three players to a course (for a larger group, assign two or three players to start at each "wicket"). Design a croquet course by placing two cones a foot apart to make wickets. The wickets should be in a scattered formation around the gym or play area. Players establish a striking order.

The game begins with each player, in turn, striking the puck toward a wicket. Each player gets one hit per turn unless they hit the other player's puck or the puck passes through a wicket. For each wicket and/or puck hit, they are awarded an extra hit. Players must pass the puck through the wickets in the correct direction to earn extra hits. The first player to complete the course is the winner.

For older players, consider adding more distance between the wickets to make the game even more challenging.

Hockey Horse

Introduction: Hockey Horse borrows the same rules and strategy of basketball Horse. A variety of shots from any distance can be practiced in this fun game.

Number of Players: 2

Suggested Grade Levels: 3rd–8th grades

Equipment: 1 hockey stick for each player, 1 puck, 1 cone

How to Play: Assign two players to a play area. One cone is placed in the middle of the play area. Each player begins with a hockey stick. Players also establish a shooting order before play can begin.

To start, the first player strikes the puck from anywhere in the play area and attempts to hit the cone. If successful, the next player must also make a goal from the exact same spot. If the second player fails to hit the cone, he or she is given the letter H. If the player hits the cone, no letter is given. After the second player has had a turn, the first player regains the puck and can take a shot from anywhere. Again, if successful, the other player must imitate it. If the first player misses the cone, the second player then has the opportunity to take a shot from anywhere in the play area. The objective is to make a shot and hope that the next player misses, causing the letters H-O-R-S-E to be spelled against him or her.

Floor Hockey Golf

Introduction: Floor Hockey Golf develops striking skills while using the strategies and scoring of golf.

Number of Players: 4-6

Suggested Grade Levels: 4th–8th grades

Equipment: 1 hockey stick for each player, 1 puck, 9 bowling pins

How to Play: Assign two or three players to a course (for a larger group, assign two or three players to start at each hole). Design a golf course by placing a numbered bowling pin (1 through 9) in a scattered formation around the gym or play area. Players establish a striking order. If needed, give each player a scorecard and pencil.

The game begins with each player, in turn, striking the puck toward Hole #1, trying to knock the bowling pin over or make contact with it. The number of shots needed to make the "Hole" is recorded. When finished, the group moves to Hole #2 and each player continues to strike the bowling pin in as few attempts possible. The objective is to finish the course by having the lowest score (that is, the fewest shot attempts).

Variation: For older players, consider adding obstacles around the course to make the game even more challenging. These can items like tumbling mats, storage containers, balls, and so forth.

Hockey Keep Away

Introduction: Playing any type of "keep away" game is always exciting for children, and this activity is no different. The hockey skills of passing and fielding are the primary skills developed.

Number of Players: 5–6

Suggested Grade Levels: 3rd–8th grades

Equipment: 1 hockey stick for each player, 1 puck

How to Play: Form a group of 5-6 players. Players stand in a circular formation with one player in the middle. All players begin with a hockey stick with one of the circular players also having the puck.

On a starting signal, the circle players begin passing and fielding the puck back and forth, while at the same time, the middle player attempts to steal it away with his or her stick. If the middle player is successful, he or she switches place with the last player who last passed or controlled the puck. Also, any player making an errand pass or not fielding the puck (causing it to exit the circle) has to switch place with the middle player. The objective for the circle players is to keep the player in the middle from touching the puck, and to avoid becoming the middle player.

Hockey Hounds & Hare

Introduction: This tag-type game develops the hockey skills of passing and fielding. The combination of using hockey skills with the fun of playing tag has proven to be a student favorite.

Number of Players: 3–5

Suggested Grade Levels: 5th–8th grades

Equipment: 1 hockey stick for each player, 1 foam puck, marking tape or cones

How to Play: Hockey Hounds & Hare is best played with 3-5 participants. With the exception of one player (the Hare), the players start in a scattered formation in a marked off area about 10' x 10' in size. Select one player to start with the puck, and one player to start in the middle of the box as the Hare. With the exception of the Hare, the player with the foam puck and all other players are called "Hounds." For safety reasons, it's highly recommended that only a foam puck be used.

On a starting signal, the players (Hounds) pass the puck back and forth attempting to tag the Hare with the puck. A tag is accomplished by having the puck touch the Hare's hockey stick or feet. The Hound with the puck cannot run or walk—a pivot is the only movement allowed. Hounds without the ball should move into a position close enough to the Hare to receive a pass. The key is for the Hounds to pass quickly and move as soon they pass the puck (the "give and go" concept). If a successful tag is made, the Hare trades places with the Hound who tagged him or her. The objective for the Hare is to last as long as possible without becoming a Hound.

Football
Games

Football Bamboozle

Introduction: This fun game contains the chasing and fleeing aspect of football, and gives children the opportunity to practice huddling, stance positions, starting signals, and score touchdowns.

Number of Players: 6

Suggested Grade Levels: 1st–5th grades

Equipment: 1 coin, 4 cones, football flags for each player

How to Play: With cones, mark off a rectangular-shaped play area. The two cones at each end form a goal line. Form two equal teams with three players each. All players are to wear football flags. Designate one team to start on offense at one goal line. The defensive team stands at the opposite goal line. Give a small coin (the "football") to one of the offensive players.

The game starts with the offensive team forming a huddle. The offensive players decide who will carry the football (that is, the coin) first. Before breaking the huddle, all of the offensive players close both fists so that the defensive players cannot determine who has the football. Both teams then assume a 3-point stance on their goal lines. When one of the offensive players calls out "ready, set, hike," the offensive players run toward the opponent's goal line with the defensive players also running forward and attempting to pull their flags. Once an offensive player has his or her flag pulled, that player must stop running and immediately reveal if he or she has the football. A touchdown is scored if the player with the football successfully crosses the goal line without having his or her flag pulled. After each play, the teams reverse roles and play continues.

Football Blocker Tag

Introduction: This high energy game is a modification of Triangle Tag. This version contains the element of blocking that is used in football and also requires quick lateral movements. The skill of "faking" can also be introduced with this fun game.

Number of Players: 4

Suggested Grade Levels: K–5th grades

Equipment: Football flags for each player

How to Play: Organize four players to a group and have each player put on football flags. Assign three players to hold hands and make a circle. The fourth player is the "tackler" and he or she stands outside the circle.

The game begins with the tackler choosing a circle player to "tackle" (that is, pull their flag). The other two circle players become "blockers" for the chosen player. The blockers work together moving laterally in the circle by sliding to the right or to the left to prevent that player from having their flag pulled. At no time can any of the circle players let go of their hands or run away from their play area. The tackler must pull the chosen players' flags by circling to the right or left, and is not allowed to go over or under the circle to make a tackle. When the chosen player has been tackled, the two players change roles. The new tackler should chase someone who has not been chased or who hasn't been chased for a while.

Football Duel

Introduction: Since there are only two participants, Football Duel maximizes ball contact opportunities and skill development. Additionally, the simple rules of this game make it a perfect choice for younger players.

Number of Players: 2

Suggested Grade Levels: K–5th grades

Equipment: Football flags for each player, 2 cones, 1 football, 1 kicking tee

How to Play: With the cones, mark off a rectangular shaped play area. The two cones at the ends represent the goal lines. There are no boundary lines. Both players start on their own goal line with each wearing football flags. Designate one player to kickoff and the other to receive the ball first.

The game begins with the kicker (the defensive player) kicking off a tee toward the receiver (the offensive player). The receiver attempts to catch or retrieve the ball and run with it past the opposite goal line without having a flag pulled by the kicking player. If successful, the receiver scores a touchdown worth six points. The players switch roles after each play.

Variation: Instead of kicking, players can substitute a punt when performing the kickoff.

Football Doubles

Introduction: Football Doubles is a natural progression of Football Duel (one-on-one football). The low number of participants requires maximum effort and concentration.

Number of Players: 4

Suggested Grade Levels: 3rd–6th grades

Equipment: Football flags for each player, 4 cones, 1 football, 1 kicking tee

How to Play: With the cones, mark off a rectangular shaped play area. The two cones at the ends represent the goal lines. There are no boundary lines. Organize two teams of two players each, with each player wearing football flags. Both teams start by facing each other on opposite goal lines. Designate one team to kickoff (defense) and the other to receive the ball first (offense).

The game begins with the defensive team kicking the football toward the receiving team (that is, the offensive team). A player on the receiving team attempts to catch or retrieve the ball and run with it past the opposite goal line without having a flag pulled by the kicking team. If successful, the receiving team scores a touchdown worth six points. However, if tackled, the ball is downed at that spot and now the offensive team has one down to score. One of the offensive players would be the quarterback and the other player is both the hiker and pass receiver. The defensive team has one defensive back to cover the receiver, and one pass rusher (who must wait for five seconds to rush the quarterback). After the play, the teams reverse roles with a new kickoff.

Football Triplets

Introduction: Football Triplets solves the problem of not having an even number of participants since it requires exactly three players. It also enhances all of the skills of regular flag football.

Number of Players: 3

Suggested Grade Levels: 3rd–6th grades

Equipment: Football flags for each player, 4 cones, 1 football, 1 kicking tee

How to Play: With the cones, mark off a rectangular shaped play area. The two cones at the ends represent the goal lines. There are no boundary lines. All three players are to wear football flags that can be easily pulled, and are to determine a kicking order before starting play. The player designated to kick first stands at one goal line ready to kick off to the other two players (the offensive players).

The kicker begins the game by kicking the football toward the receiving team (that is, the two offensive players). A player on the receiving team attempts to catch or retrieve the ball and run with it past the opposite goal line without having a flag pulled by the kicker. If successful, the offensive team scores a touchdown worth six points. However, if tackled, the ball is downed at that spot and now the offensive team has one down to score. One of the offensive players would be the quarterback and the other player is both the hiker and pass receiver. The kicker becomes the lone defensive player and his/her job is to cover the receiver. The quarterback has to pass (no running downfield), and only has ten seconds to get the pass off. If the offensive team successfully scores a touchdown, both players are awarded six points. After the play, the players rotate with the next designated kicker kicking off to restart the game.

Football One Hundred

Introduction: Football One Hundred develops the flag football skills of passing, catching, hiking, and pass defense.

Number of Players: 4

Suggested Grade Levels: 3rd–8th grades

Equipment: 1 football

How to Play: The four players start by assuming a starting position as the quarterback, center, receiver, or pass defender. The receiver lines up in a three-point stance next to the center, the defender faces the receiver, the center begins with the football, and the quarterback stands about 6 feet behind the center.

The quarterback begins by yelling out Ready, Set, Hike." On the word "Hike," the center hikes the ball to the quarterback and the receiver runs downfield to catch a pass. The defender should stay as close as possible to the receiver trying to prevent the pass from being completed. The receiver is awarded ten points if he or she successfully makes a catch. However, the pass defender is awarded ten points if he or she is able to intercept the pass. An incomplete pass is not worth any points. Players rotate positions after each play. The quarterback moves to receiver, the receiver to pass defender, the pass defender to center, and the center becomes the next quarterback. The objective is to be the first player to reach one hundred points.

Football Twenty-One

Introduction: The strategy of this game is similar to the basketball game of Twenty-One (that is, the player objective is to score exactly twenty-one points). Football Twenty-One develops the skills of passing, catching, hiking, and playing pass defense.

Number of Players: 4

Suggested Grade Levels: 3rd–8th grades

Equipment: 1 football, 6 cones

How to Play: With the cones, set up a play area as shown in the illustration. The individual zones should be spaced about 5-10 yards apart. Form two teams of two players each. The two players on offense start by assuming a starting position as the quarterback and center/receiver. The center begins with the football, and the quarterback stands about 6 feet behind the center. The two players on defense are pass defenders and stand a few feet away facing the center/receiver.

The quarterback begins by yelling out Ready, Set, Hike." On the word "Hike," the center hikes the ball to the quarterback and runs downfield to catch a pass. The defenders should stay as close as possible to the receiver trying to prevent the pass from being completed. The offensive team is awarded a certain number of points for a successful catch. The exact number of points will depend on the zone the receiver was in at the time of the reception (receivers cannot run with the ball after the catch). An incomplete pass is not worth any points. The offensive team has only one play on offense and both teams must switch after each play. The objective is to be the first team to reach exactly twenty-one points. The offensive team should rotate positions throughout the game.

Ultimate Football

Introduction: This fast-action game is played somewhat like the game of Frisbee Ultimate, with the exception that a football replaces the use of a frisbee. Passing, catching, and defensive play are the principle skills developed.

Number of Players: 6

Suggested Grade Levels: 4rd–8th grades

Equipment: 4 cones, 1 football, player identification vests

How to Play: With the cones, mark off a rectangular shaped play area. The two cones at the ends represent the goal lines. Organize two teams of three players each. Both teams start by facing each other on in the middle of the play area. Designate one team to start on defense and the other team to start on offense with the football. Each player should choose an opposing player to guard throughout the game.

The team objective is to have a player catch a pass past the opponent's goal line for a score (six points). The player on offense with the football starts the game by passing to teammate. Since players with possession of the football cannot run with it, the ball is advanced down the field by a combination of completed passes. Upon catching a pass, a player has only two steps to come to a complete stop or else a violation is called. Additionally, passers have only five seconds to throw the ball or a violation is also called. A violation results in the other team taking possession of the football at that spot, and they now try to advance the ball offensively toward the opposite goal line. As long as the offensive team successfully catches the football, they have an unlimited number of plays to score. Besides the violations mentioned above, any thrown or dropped ball that touches the ground (an "incomplete" pass) also results in the other team taking possession.

One Down

Introduction: This easy-to-understand game provides players plenty of opportunities to play both offense and defense. Passing, catching, hiking, and defensive play are the principle skills developed.

Number of Players: 6

Suggested Grade Levels: 4rd–8th grades

Equipment: 4 cones, 1 football, football flags for each player

How to Play: With the cones, mark off a rectangular shaped play area. The two cones at the ends represent the goal lines. Organize two teams of three players each. Both teams start by facing each other on in the middle of the play area (there are no kickoffs). Designate one team to start on defense and the other team to start on offense with the football. The offensive team consists of a quarterback and two receivers (one who also doubles as the center). The defensive players are all pass defenders and line up facing the offensive team.

The offensive team starts with the ball in the center of the play area, and they have one down to score. After the hike, both the receiver and the center go downfield to catch the pass from the quarterback. When a player receives a pass (or is handed the ball on a lateral), he or she runs toward the opponent's goal line trying to score a touchdown. Defensive players attempt to pull a player's flag to stop play (the ball carrier is considered "tackled" at that spot). The opponents are given possession at the spot of any dead ball (or a tackle or incomplete pass), and they now start with one offensive down going the opposite direction. A touchdown is scored each time a ball carrier crosses the opponent's goal line with the ball or catches a pass past the goal line. After each touchdown, the non-scoring team starts on offense at midfield.

Shake & Bake

Introduction: This high energy game contains the element of faking and eluding a defender that is used in football. The primary objective is to improve the skills of passing, catching, faking, and pass defense.

Number of Players: 6

Suggested Grade Levels: 4th–8th grades

Equipment: 1 football, identification vests, 4 cones

How to Play: Shake & Bake can be played indoors using the line markings of a half basketball court, or outdoors with the cones marking a square-shaped play area. Form two equal teams of three players each. Before starting, each player should choose an opponent to guard. Designate one team to start with the football.

The objective for the team with the football (the offensive team) is to complete five consecutive passes to score one point. The game begins a player on offense passing to a teammate from anywhere within the play area. A successful catch counts as the first of the five passes and catches needed. With each subsequent completed pass, players count out loud. Offensive players will need to make quick faking movements in order to get away from the defensive player guarding them. During play, the football may not be passed back to the person who just passed it, nor can a player in possession of the ball take more than three steps. Pivoting, as in basketball, is only movement allowed after coming to a stop. Defensive players cannot take the ball from the hands of an offensive player, nor can they make any physical contact with a passer or receiver. If a pass is intercepted, missed, or fumbled away, the other team takes immediate possession and they attempt to score by making five consecutive passes and catches. Also, after each successful score, the non-scoring team takes possession.

Capture the Footballs

Introduction: This student favorite is very similar to the popular game of Capture the Flag, except now the players are trying to bring footballs over to their side instead of a flag.

Number of Players: 6

Suggested Grade Levels: 4th–8th grades

Equipment: 6 footballs, football flags for each player, cones, 1 long tug-o-war rope, 6 large hula hoops

How to Play: With the cones, design a rectangular-shaped play area. Place the tug-o-war rope at midfield to divide the play area into two halves. Also, with cones, mark a prisoner's area in each half. Place three large hula hoops randomly spaced apart on each side, and put one football in the middle of each one. Form two teams of three players each. All of the players wear flag football flags for pulling. Each team starts play on their designated side.

On a starting signal, the players cross the midfield line and attempt to steal a football from their opponents without getting a flag pulled. A player stealing a football can only run it past the midfield line and cannot pass or kick it across. The football must be placed back into the hula hoop if the player has his or her flag pulled before making it safely past the midfield line. Each stolen football is given to the instructor. The objective is to be the first team to give all three of the opponent's footballs to the instructor. Any player who has his or her flag pulled while in the opponent's territory must go to their prison. However, a prisoner can be set free if a teammate makes it safely into the prison, and walks the player back (hands held high). Also, at any time, the instructor can yell out "jail break," to release all prisoners.

Football Triathlon

Introduction: The "punt, pass, kick" format of this fun activity simulates a triathlon event while improving cardiovascular endurance at the same time.

Number of Players: 2

Suggested Grade Levels: 3rd–8th grades

Equipment: 2 footballs, 2 kicking tees, cones

How to Play: With the cones, design a cross country course. This game can also be played using a football field. If using a football field, the players would travel back and forth between the goal lines. The players begin with a partner, and each player has his or her own football and tee. The tees are set by the second cone. Each pair stands on the starting line with a football in hand.

On a starting signal, each player throws the football as far as possible toward the first cone. He or she then runs to the spot of the dead ball and immediately throws it again toward the first cone. No player is allowed to run or walk with the ball. After reaching the first cone, the players take their kicking tee and kick as far as possible toward the second cone. After reaching the second cone, the players drop their kicking tee and now punt as far as possible toward the finish line. Play continues in this fashion until each player has punted the football past the finish line. The objective is to finish the course as quickly as possible.

Football Horse Race

Introduction: This exciting game involves hiking a football and racing against other players.

Number of Players: 6

Suggested Grade Levels: 3rd–5th grades

Equipment: 1 football for each pair of players

How to Play: Organize the players into pairs. The players decide who is going to start as the hiker and who will be the runner (or horse). The hikers stand on the inside of the circle and assume a centering position with the football. Each runner stands a few feet away from their hiker and assumes a quarterback-like stance.

The instructor begins by calling out "Ready, Set, Hike." On Hike, the inside players hike the football in a shotgun formation to their teammate who is awaiting the football (like a quarterback would). The hiker does not run—rather, he or she stand with feet apart in a stationary position. Meanwhile, the receiving teammate (the Horse) catches the ball and runs with it clockwise around the outside of the stationary players. After arriving back to his her teammate (the hiker), the Horse crawls through the legs of the hiker and sits on the inside circle. The objective is to be the first Horse to arrive back and sitting. Have teammates switch roles after each race.

Football Express

Introduction: This activity is much like Pony Express (a popular running game), except now the four players are hiking a football and running.

Number of Players: 4

Suggested Grade Levels: 3rd–8th grades

Equipment: 1 football, 4 cones

How to Play: With the cones, design a square shaped play area. The four cones should be about 6-8 feet apart. Form a team of four players, and assign each of the players to a cone. The player at cone #1 begins with a football.

On a starting signal, the player at cone #1 hikes the football (shotgun style) to the teammate at cone #2, then runs forward to cone #2. The player at cone #2 catches the hiked ball and immediately snaps the ball to the teammate at cone #3, then runs forward to cone #3. The player at cone #3 snaps the ball to the player at cone #4, and then runs forward to cone #4. The player at cone #4 has to run to cone #1 before hiking to the teammate at cone #2. Players continue hiking the ball in this fashion until all of the players are back in their original starting positions. The objective is to continuously get faster with each race. With a large group of players, consider having multiple teams of four players compete against each other.

Punting Touchdowns

Introduction: This activity gives players a chance to practice the skill of punting in a challenging and fun setting.

Number of Players: 2

Suggested Grade Levels: 3rd–8th grades

Equipment: 2 footballs, 4 cones

How to Play: With the cones, design a long rectangular shaped play area. The goal lines are at the far ends of the play area. This game can also be played using a football field. If using a football field, the players would travel back and forth between the goal lines. The players begin with a partner, and each pair is given a football. Players can use a coin toss or perform a quick rock-paper-scissors to determine who will punt first.

The first punter begins the game by punting from midfield as far as possible toward the opponent's goal line. The receiving partner attempts to catch the ball, or at least tries to retrieve the ball to prevent any bouncing of it toward his or her own goal line. The receiving partner then punts it back, trying to angle it over the head of the first punter and toward the opponent's goal line. The objective is to be the first player to punt the ball (either in the air or on the bounce) past the opponent's goal line.

Four Downs

Introduction: This three-on-three player game is a natural progression of Football Doubles (see page 59). All of the major skills of flag football are developed in this activity.

Number of Players: 6

Suggested Grade Levels: 4rd–8th grades

Equipment: 4 cones, 1 football, 1 kicking tee, football flags for each player

How to Play: With the cones, mark off a rectangular shaped play area. The two cones at the ends represent the goal lines. Organize two teams of three players each. Both teams start by facing each other on opposite goal lines. Designate one team to start on defense and the other team to start on offense with the football. The offensive team consists of a quarterback and two receivers (one who also doubles as the center). The defensive players are all pass defenders and line up facing the offensive team.

The defensive team starts the game with a kickoff from its goal line. One of the offensive players catches or retrieves the kicked ball and attempts to run it past the opponent's goal line without having a flag pulled. If the runner is tackled (that is, has a flag pulled), the ball is downed at that spot and the offensive team has three downs to score. The offensive team attempts to advance the ball toward the opponent's goal line by catching passes and running (only passing plays are allowed). Incomplete passes result in the ball staying at previous spot. After a score or after four downs if the offensive team fails to score, the teams reverse roles with a new kickoff.

Soccer
Games

Soccer Duel

Introduction: This one-on-one game maximizes dribbling opportunities and requires tremendous hustle. The simple rules and strategy makes it appropriate for all ages.

Number of Players: 2

Suggested Grade Levels: K–8th grades

Equipment: 1 soccer ball, 2 cones

How to Play: The play area consists of two cones placed approximately 15-20 feet apart. There are no boundary lines. The two players start in the middle of the two cones, with each facing the cone that they will attempt to hit with the ball. One player is designated to start with the soccer ball.

The player with the ball begins the game with a dribble. The objective is to advance the ball toward the opponent's cone in order to kick and hit the cone for a score. If successful, one point is scored and the ball is placed back in the middle for the non-scoring player to begin play again. After the kickoff, a player may attempt to steal the ball at any time to become the offensive player. Since there are boundary lines, players can shoot and hit an opponent's cone from any angle.

No player can touch the ball with his or her hands. A violation results in the other player gaining possession at the spot of the infraction.

Soccer Doubles

Introduction: This two-on-two activity is a natural progression of Soccer Duel (one-on-one soccer) and maximizes ball contact opportunities. Most of the major skills of playing soccer are utilized in this easy-to-understand and active game.

Number of Players: 4

Suggested Grade Levels: K–8th grades

Equipment: 1 soccer ball, 2 cones, player identification vests

How to Play: The play area consists of two cones placed about 20 feet apart. There are no boundary lines. Form two teams of two players each. There are no designated positions, except playing the goalie position should be limited (instead, passing and offensive teamwork should be encouraged).

This game is played much like Soccer Duel except now there are two players on each team and the skill of passing is utilized. One team starts with a kickoff in the middle of the play area. The objective is to advance the ball toward the opponent's cone in order to shoot and hit the cone for a score. If successful, one point is scored and the ball is brought back to the middle for a kickoff by the non-scoring team. Defensive players may attempt to steal the puck at any time to gain possession. Since there are no boundary lines, players can shoot and hit an opponent's cone from any angle.

As in regular soccer, no player can use his or her hands. A violation results in the other team gaining possession of the puck at the spot of the infraction.

Mini Soccer

Introduction: This three-on-three activity is a natural progression of Soccer Duel (one-on-one soccer) and Soccer Doubles (two-on-two soccer). All of the major skills of playing soccer are enhanced with this high-energy game.

Number of Players: 6

Suggested Grade Levels: K–8th grades

Equipment: 1 soccer ball, 2 small soccer goals (or use cones), player identification vests

How to Play: The play area consists of two goals about 30 feet apart. If two soccer nets are not available for goals, consider substituting two cones about 5 feet apart at each end. There are no boundary lines. Form two teams of three players each. Designate two forwards and one goalie on each team.

This game is played much like Soccer Doubles except now there are three players on each team and the position of goalie is introduced. The game begins with one kicking off in the middle of the play area. The offensive team's objective is to control the ball and advance it toward the opponent's goal in order to kick the ball into the goal for a score. If successful, one point is scored and the ball is brought back to the middle for a kickoff by the non-scoring team. Defensive players may attempt to steal the puck at any time to gain possession. Since there are no boundary lines, players can shoot and score from any angle (including backwards through the two cones). Have teammates rotate positions throughout the game.

Besides the goalie, no player is allowed to use hands. A violation results in the other team gaining possession of the ball at the spot of the infraction.

One Goal Soccer

Introduction: This one-on-one game improves dribbling skills, and requires a lot of hustle and energy.

Number of Players: 2

Suggested Grade Levels: K–8th grades

Equipment: 1 soccer ball, 2 cones

How to Play: The play area consists of two cones placed approximately 6 feet apart for the one goal that exist in this game. There are no boundary lines. The players start about 20 feet from the goal, with one player designated to start with the soccer ball.

The player with the ball begins the game with a dribble. The objective is to advance the ball toward the goal in order to dribble or pass the ball through the cones for a score. If successful, one point is scored and the ball is placed back at the top of the play area for the non-scoring player to begin play again. After the kickoff, a player may attempt to steal the ball at any time to become the offensive player. Since there are boundary lines, players can shoot and score from either side of the goal.

No player can touch the ball with his or her hands. A violation results in the other player gaining possession at the spot of the infraction.

Goal Line Soccer

Introduction: Instead of using a traditional soccer goal, players score in this game by passing the ball to a teammate who traps it on the opponent's end line.

Number of Players: 6

Suggested Grade Levels: 3rd–8th grades

Equipment: 1 soccer ball, 4 cones, player identification vests

How to Play: With the cones, mark off a square-shaped play area. The end lines between the cones represent the goal lines. Form two teams of three players each. Each team is assigned to defend an goal line. Designate two players from each team to start as defenders near their goal line, while the remaining player (the "target") starts on the goal line opposite of his or her teammates. Designate one team to start on offense with the ball.

The team with the ball begins the game by passing to each other and advancing it toward the opponent's end line. Their objective is to pass it to the target teammate who is standing on the opponent's end line. A score is made if the target player traps the ball cleanly on the end line or within a few feet of the line. Defending players try to prevent opponents from completing a pass to the target player. A change of possession occurs if the ball is stolen; the ball goes out of bounds past the target player; or after a score.

Have the target players switch off periodically with their infield teammates so that everyone gets an opportunity to play as the target.

Soccer Twins

Introduction: Soccer Twins calls for the two players on each team to form "three-legged" teams, and compete against each other in a game that offers lots of fun and laughter.

Number of Players: 4

Suggested Grade Levels: 3rd–8th grades

Equipment: 1 soccer ball, 2 soccer goals (or substitute 4 cones for the goals), flag football belts (for strapping legs together)

How to Play: The play area consists of two small soccer goals placed about 30 feet apart. There are no boundary lines. Form two teams of two players each. Using the football belts, the two teammates strap their inside legs together to form a "three-legged team." There are no designated positions.

This game is played much like Soccer Doubles except now the players on each team form two three-legged teams. The "twins" designated to start with the ball begin by with a dribble in the middle of the play area. The objective is to control the ball and advance it toward the opponent's goal in order to kick it in the net for a score. If successful, one point is scored and the ball is brought back to the middle for another kickoff. Defensive players may attempt to steal the ball at any time to gain possession. Using hands is not allowed. A violation results in the other team gaining possession of the ball at the spot of the infraction.

Soccer Pirates

Introduction: Soccer Pirates is a highly engaged game that enhances the soccer skills of ball control, dribbling, and stealing.

Number of Players: 4

Suggested Grade Levels: 3rd–8th grades

Equipment: 4 soccer balls, 5 hula hoops for outdoor play (marking tape for inside play)

How to Play: Place four hula hoops in a square-shaped formation about 20-30 feet apart, and one hula hoop in the middle. If playing inside, use marking tape to make 5 circles (about 4 feet in diameter). Place all four soccer balls in the middle hoop. Each player stands inside one of the four corner hoops.

On a starting signal, all four players move toward the center circle, take one soccer ball with their feet, and dribble it back toward their circle (placing it inside the hoop). At this point, each player attempts to steal a ball from another hoop while guarding against his/her own ball being stolen. The objective is to be the first player to have two soccer balls inside his/her circle.

Variation: For three player groups, set up a triangular shaped play area with one hoop in the middle. The same rules as described above would still apply.

Soccer Horse

Introduction: Soccer Horse borrows the same rules and strategy of its basketball version. A variety of shots from any distance can be practiced in this fun game.

Number of Players: 2

Suggested Grade Levels: K–8th grades

Equipment: 1 soccer ball, 1 soccer goal (or substitute a cone)

How to Play: Assign two players to a play area with one soccer goal. If a goal is not available, substitute a cone (players would then be aiming for the cone). Players also establish a shooting order before play can begin.

To start, the first player kicks the soccer ball from anywhere in the play area and attempts to make it go into the goal. If successful, the next player must also make a goal from the exact same spot. If the second player fails to score, he or she is given the letter H. No letter is given to the second player if he or she successfully scores. After the second player has had a turn, the first player regains the ball and can take a shot from anywhere. Again, if successful, the other player must imitate it. If the first player misses the goal, the second player then has the opportunity to take a shot from anywhere in the play area. The objective is to make a goal and hope that the next player misses, causing the letters H-O-R-S-E to be spelled against him or her.

Dribbling Marbles

Introduction: Soccer Marbles creates a lot of fun while practicing dribbling skills. It also builds cardiovascular fitness with its constant movement.

Number of Players: 3-6

Suggested Grade Levels: 2nd–6th grades

Equipment: 1 soccer ball for each player, 4 or more cones

How to Play: With the cones, design a square-shaped play area of about 30 feet by 30 feet. Each player starts with a soccer ball and stands anywhere within the play area.

On a starting signal, the players start dribbling. While avoiding the other players' soccer balls, the players see how many times they can make their ball touch another ball while still keeping control. Have the players keep track of how many times their ball touches another ball (a "bump"). Play several one minute rounds and challenge the players to improve their numbers with each round.

Soccer Bandit

Introduction: Soccer Bandit is a chasing and fleeing game that enhances the skills of dribbling and stealing. The non-stop action also builds cardiovascular fitness.

Number of Players: 2

Suggested Grade Levels: K–6th grades

Equipment: 1 soccer ball

How to Play: This one-on-one game is best played outside on a square-shaped play area of about 20 feet by 20 feet. If several games are being played simultaneously, it might be best to mark off designated play areas for each pair of players. Assign one player to start with the soccer ball, and the other player begins as the Bandit (or ball stealer).

On a starting signal, the Bandit chases the player with the soccer ball and attempts to steal it away. A player who loses the ball becomes the new Bandit. The objective for the player with the ball is to dribble and last as long as possible without becoming a Bandit. The Bandit cannot touch the other player while attempting a steal.

Soccer Hounds & Hare

Introduction: This tag game develops the soccer skills of passing and trapping. The combination of using soccer skills with the fun of eluding and/or making a tag has proven to be a student favorite.

Number of Players: 3–5

Suggested Grade Levels: 5th–8th grades

Equipment: 1 foam soccer ball, marking tape or cones

How to Play: Hockey Hounds & Hare is best played with 3-5 participants. With the exception of one player (the Hare), the players start in a scattered formation in a marked off area about 10' x 10' in size. Select one player to start with the foam soccer ball, and one player to start in the middle of the box as the Hare. With the exception of the Hare, the player with the foam ball and all other players are called "Hounds." For safety reasons, it's highly recommended that only a foam soccer ball be used.

On a starting signal, the players (Hounds) pass the ball back and forth attempting to tag the Hare with the ball. A tag is accomplished by having the ball touch the Hare's feet. The Hound with the ball cannot dribble—he or she can only pass and trap the ball. Hounds without the ball should move into a position close enough to the Hare to receive a pass. The key is for the Hounds to pass quickly and move as soon they pass the ball (the "give and go" concept). If a successful tag is made, the Hare trades places with the Hound who tagged him or her with the ball. The objective for the Hare is to last as long as possible without becoming a Hound.

Soccer Flag Tag

Introduction: This tag game develops the soccer skill of dribbling in a fun setting that requires a lot of movement.

Number of Players: 3–6

Suggested Grade Levels: 4th–8th grades

Equipment: 1 soccer ball and flag set for each player, marking tape (or cones)

How to Play: With the cones (or marking tape if playing inside), mark off a square-shaped play area about 30 feet by 30 feet in size. Soccer Flag Tag is best played with 3-6 participants. The players each start with a soccer ball and a flag that is tucked into the back of their pants (at least half of the flag should be hanging out).

The game begins with the players dribbling among themselves. Each player's objective is to dribble after other players and steal their flags while also keeping his or her own flag from being pulled. Players hold the stolen flags in their hands while dribbling about. Players should dribble the ball under control throughout the game and are not permitted to abandon the ball to chase after another player. The player who ends up with the highest number of stolen flags while keeping his or her own flag wins the contest.

Soccer Bowling

Introduction: Soccer Bowling develops kicking accuracy while using the terminology and scoring of playing regular bowling.

Number of Players: 2

Suggested Grade Levels: K–6th grades

Equipment: 1 soccer ball, 10 bowling pins

How to Play: Set up a "bowling lane" with the 10 bowling pins approximately 30 feet from the spot where the kicker stands. This distance can vary depending on the age and skill level of the players. One player stands behind the pins ready to set back up any knocked over pins, and the other player stands ready to kick.

Soccer Bowling is essentially the game of bowling with a ball being kicked instead of rolled. The first bowler attempts to kick and knock down as many pins as possible. The objective is to gain a strike by knocking all of the pins down, or to knock over as many as possible by the second kick. After the second kick, the bowler switches with the pin set-up player. Each bowler is allowed two kicks per frame, with 10 frames in each game. Scoring is the same as in bowling.

Soccer Knockout

Introduction: The objectives of playing Soccer Knockout are to develop dribbling, shielding, and poke tackling skills. Additionally, cardiovascular fitness is enhanced because of the non-stop action.

Number of Players: 3-6

Suggested Grade Levels: 2nd–8th grades

Equipment: 1 soccer ball for each player, 4 or more cones

How to Play: With the cones, design a square-shaped play area of about 30 feet by 30 feet. Each player starts with a soccer ball and stands anywhere within the play area.

On a starting signal, the players start dribbling randomly within the area attempting to kick other players' balls out of the area while, at the same time, maintaining possession of their own ball. A player whose ball is kicked or poked outside the play area cannot retrieve it. Instead, he or she can only attempt to knock other players' balls away until the game ends. The game ends when only one player remains in possession of his or her ball. Play several rounds.

Variation: Consider having the players who lose their ball retrieve and reenter the game over and over. Assess one point each time to the player who has his or her ball knocked out. At the end of a timed round, the player with the fewest points wins.

Soccer Golf

Introduction: Soccer Golf develops kicking skills while using the strategies and scoring of playing golf.

Number of Players: 2-3

Suggested Grade Levels: 4th–8th grades

Equipment: 1 soccer ball for each player, 9 hula hoops, 9 numbered cones

How to Play: Assign two or three players to a course (for a larger group, assign two or three players to start at each hole). Design a golf course by placing the hula hoops with a numbered cone inside (1 through 9) in a scattered formation around the gym or play area. Players establish a striking order. If needed, give each player a scorecard and pencil.

The game begins with each player, in turn, kicking the ball toward hole #1, trying to land it inside the hula hoop. The number of shots needed to make the "hole" is recorded for each player. When finished, the group moves to hole #2 and each player continues to kick and land the ball inside the hula hoop in as few attempts possible. The objective is to finish the course by having the lowest score (that is, the fewest kick attempts).

Open Goal Challenge

Introduction: This active game allows players to practice dribbling at full speed with vision and ball control. The racing aspect of this game adds an additional element of fun.

Number of Players: 6

Suggested Grade Levels: 4th–8th grades

Equipment: 4 soccer balls, 8 cones

How to Play: With the cones, design four 3-foot wide mini-goals (see illustration below). Designate a starting line about 30-60 feet away from the goals. Position two players (the "Its") to stand in the center of the play area. The other four players are stationed, each with a ball, on the starting line.

On a starting signal, the two "It" players who do not have soccer balls sprint to the mini soccer goals and each takes a position in one of the mini-goals as act as blockers. At the same time, the dribblers on the starting line, each with a ball, dribble as fast as can across the play area and through an open goal. A goal is considered blocked once a dribbler goes through it, and no other dribbler may go through it. The two dribblers left out become the new Its. The objective is to avoid being an It.

Soccer Star

Introduction: Soccer Star is played much like the basketball game of The Moving Star (see page 32). However, in this version, the soccer skills of passing and trapping are being emphasized. It is also a great cardiovascular workout!

Number of Players: 5

Suggested Grade Levels: 4th–8th grades

Equipment: 1 soccer ball

How to Play: The Moving Star is played with five participants. The players start in a circular formation as shown in the illustration. Select one player (player #1) to start with the soccer ball.

Before play, have the players practice passing the ball in a "star" pattern as shown in the illustration. The player with the soccer ball (#1) passes to player #2. Player #2 traps it and passes to player #3, and so on. The "star" pattern continues until the ball gets back to where it started. Once the group has mastered the pattern, add the "moving" part. After player #1 passes the ball, he or she immediately runs counterclockwise around the outside of the circle to his/her original spot. Each subsequent player receiving a pass immediately runs in the same fashion (after passing the ball first). The objective is for each runner to arrive back to his/her original spot before the ball gets there.

Soccer Speedsters

Introduction: This fun and competitive activity improves dribbling speed and develops aerobic endurance.

Number of Players: Unlimited pairs

Suggested Grade Levels: 2nd–8th grades

Equipment: 1 soccer ball and 2 cones for each pair of students

How to Play: Place two cones about 30-60 feet apart for each pair of players. One cone represents the starting line and the other cone is the turnaround spot. Each player teams up with a partner and both stand by the starting cone. The first player in each line starts with the soccer ball.

On a starting signal, the first player of each pair dribbles at full speed to the turnaround cone and dribbles back to the starting cone as fast as possible. This player then traps it at the starting cone so his or her partner can now dribble at top speed down and back. The first pair to finish the race wins. Run multiple races with short breaks in between for maximum endurance training. At any time, consider adjusting the race distance to accommodate the skill level and ages of the players.

Soccer Juggling

Introduction: This is a great choice as either a warm-up or a cool-down activity. Juggling a soccer ball requires quick actions, focus, and teamwork.

Number of Players: 2-4

Suggested Grade Levels: 4th–8th grades

Equipment: 1 soccer ball

How to Play: Soccer Juggling can be played with two or more participants. The players start by facing each other or stand in a circular formation as shown in the illustration. Select one player to start with the soccer ball.

The group objective is to work together to get as many consecutive juggles in a row before the ball lands on the ground. A player with the ball begins by heading the ball to a teammate, dropping a ball to his or her feet and passing it to a teammate in the air, or dropping the ball to the thighs and passing the ball upward to a teammate. The players then attempt to keep the ball in the air by passing and receiving the ball with various body surfaces (head, thigh, chest, and feet). Challenge the group to go as long as possible with as few drops possible in a one minute contest.

Using Your Head

Introduction: This is a great game for having players practice the heading technique that is used to score goals.

Number of Players: 3

Suggested Grade Levels: 4th–8th grades

Equipment: 1 soccer ball, soccer goal (or two cones)

How to Play: The play area consists of having a small soccer net or two cones placed about 10 feet apart to represent the goal. Position one of three players to play goalie, one to the side of the goal as the server, and one player about 12-20 feet in front of the goal as the header. The server begins with the ball.

The server begins action by underhand tossing the ball upward so that it drops near the middle between where the goalie and the header are standing. The header moves forward and attempts to score by heading the ball through the goal past the goalie. The header is awarded one point if successful. Players rotate positions after each play. The objective is to end play with the highest number of points.

Goalie Battle

Introduction: This one-on-one game gives participants the chance to practice goalkeeping skills.

Number of Players: 2

Suggested Grade Levels: 2nd–8th grades

Equipment: 1 soccer ball, 2 small soccer goals (or substitute cones to make goals)

How to Play: The play area consists of having a small soccer goal (or two cones about 10-15 feet apart) placed at each end of the play area. Depending on the age of the players, the distance between the goals can vary between 30-60 feet. Position each of the two players at the goals. Designate one of the goalies (Goalie #1) to start with the two balls.

Goalie #1 begins action by moving forward a few steps and attempts to score by kicking or throwing the ball through the goal past the goalie. Goalie #1 is awarded one point if successful. Goalies can stop the ball with either a catch or a deflection. After a goal scored or a save, Goalie #2 tries to score against Goalie #1 in the same manner. Goalies remain in their positions throughout the game. The objective is to end play with the highest number of points.

Softball Games

Softball Duel

Introduction: This one-on-one softball game maximizes skill development opportunities. The simple and easy-to-understand rules make it a terrific activity for beginners.

Number of Players: 2

Suggested Grade Levels: K–4th grades

Equipment: 1 batting tee, 1 whiffle bat, 1 whiffle ball, 2 bases

How to Play: The play area consists of two bases placed approximately 20-30 feet apart. Designate one base as the "home" base and the other as the "far" base. There are no boundary lines. The batting tee is placed to the side of the home base. One player begins at bat while the other player starts as the fielder.

The game begins with the batter hitting the ball off the tee and running to the far base and back before the fielder retrieves the ball and touches home base. One point (or "run") is awarded to the batter if he or she beats the fielder to home base. Likewise, no point is given if the fielder arrives at home base before the batter. There are no outs for tagging a runner or catching a fly ball. The players reverse roles after each play.

Variations: Older players can pitch to each other instead of using a batting tee. Another option is for batters to self-toss and hit the ball. A base running option for older players is to increase the running distance by adding a second or third base.

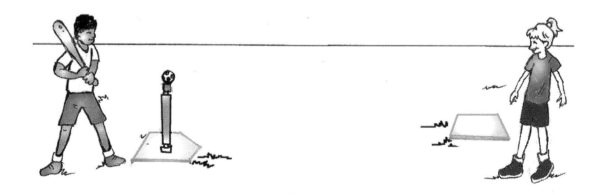

Softball Doubles

Introduction: This two-on-two activity maximizes ball handling and batting opportunities. It's a natural progression from Softball Duel, and develops all of the major skills of playing softball.

Number of Players: 4

Suggested Grade Levels: K–5th grades

Equipment: 1 batting tee, 1 whiffle bat, 1 whiffle ball, 2 bases

How to Play: The play area consists of two bases placed approximately 30-40 feet apart. Designate one base as the "home" base and the other as the "far" base. There are no boundary lines. The batting tee is placed to the side of the home base. Form two teams of two players each. One team begins at bat while the other team starts as the fielders.

The game begins with the batter hitting the ball out into the field. The batter's objective is to make it safely to the far base, where he/she can choose to stop and wait for the next batter to hit him/her home, or to the far base and back without stopping. A run is awarded each time a player runs to the far base and back to home base. A batter is put out if a fielder catches a fly ball or if tagged with the ball while running the bases. A batter can also be put out if the fielding team tags the far base before the batter arrives (which introduces the concept of the "force" out). There is no base stealing and base runners are not allowed to lead off. The teams switch places after three outs.

Variations: Older players can pitch to each other instead of using a batting tee. Another option is for batters to self-toss and hit the ball.

Softball Triplets

Introduction: This three-player game develops throwing, catching, and batting skills. It also introduces the concept of fielders working together to get a batter out.

Number of Players: 3

Suggested Grade Levels: K–4th grades

Equipment: 1 batting tee, 1 whiffle bat, 1 whiffle ball, 2 bases

How to Play: The play area consists of two bases placed approximately 30-40 feet apart. Designate one base as the "home" base and the other as the "far" base. There are no boundary lines. The batting tee is placed to the side of the home base. Designate one player to begin as the batter, one player as an infielder, and one player as the outfielder.

The game begins with the batter hitting the ball out into the field. The batter's objective is to make it safely to the far base and back to home without stopping. A run is awarded each time a player runs to the far base and back to home base. A batter is put out if a fielder catches a fly ball or if tagged with the ball while running the bases. A batter can also be put out if the fielding team tags the far base or home base before the batter arrives (which introduces the concept of two fielders working together to get a "force" out). After each play, the players rotate positions. The batter moves to outfield, the outfielder to infielder, and the infielder becomes the next batter.

Variations: Older players can pitch to each other instead of using a batting tee (that is, the fielder is also the pitcher). Another option is for batters to self-toss and hit the ball.

No Team Softball

Introduction: This unique game is played much like regular softball, except each player becomes his or her own "team." All of the skills of softball are developed.

Number of Players: 6

Suggested Grade Levels: 3rd–8th grades

Equipment: 1 batting tee, 1 whiffle bat, 1 whiffle ball, 4 bases

How to Play: The play area consists of a regular softball field with four bases. A batting tee is placed to the side of the home base. Assign one player to bat, and five players to the field in the positions of catcher, first base, shortstop, right outfield, and left outfield. Because of the limited positions, the shortstop should be instructed to take care of both second and third bases during play.

The game is played with regular softball rules except there are fewer players and they are more or less playing for themselves. Following each out, the players rotate with the player who is out going to right field. The right fielder moves to left field, left fielder to shortstop, shortstop to first base, first base to pitcher, pitcher to catcher, and the catcher becomes the next batter. A batter continues to bat and run the bases as long as he or she is not put out. Players keep track of their own score. The objective is finish the game with the highest number of runs possible.

Variations: Older players can pitch to each other instead of using a batting tee. Another option is for batters to self-toss and hit the ball.

Softball 500

Introduction: This simple game adds fun and competition to the practice of fielding both fly and ground balls. The skill of batting is also enhanced.

Number of Players: 3-5

Suggested Grade Levels: 3rd–8th grades

Equipment: 1 batting tee, 1 whiffle bat, 1 whiffle ball

How to Play: The play area consists of a large open area. A batting tee can be used for the younger or less-skilled players. The players decide a batting order. Assign player #1 to bat, and the other players to the field. An ideal number of fielders would be three or four.

The batter begins by hitting the ball off the tee toward any of the fielders. The fielders attempt to catch the batted ball without error for points. A fielder is awarded 100 points for each successful catch of either a fly hit or grounder. After each batted ball, the players rotate positions with the next designated batter coming to the tee and the batter becoming a fielder. The objective is to be the first player to reach 500 points.

Variations: Older and more highly-skilled players can self-toss and hit the ball instead of using a tee.

Pickle

Introduction: This exciting, three-player activity recreates a softball game's rundown or "pickle" —a situation in which a base runner is caught between two bases with the possibility of being tagged out by one of the two base fielders. Pickle develops the base running ability to escape a rundown situation, and it also enhances the skills of throwing and catching.

Number of Players: 3

Suggested Grade Levels: 2nd–8th grades

Equipment: 1 whiffle ball, 2 bases

How to Play: The play area consists of an open area with two bases placed approximately 30-50 feet apart. Designate two players to start on the bases as the fielders, and a third player positioned in the middle of the bases as the base runner. One of the fielders begins with the ball.

On a starting signal, the two fielders begin throwing the ball back and forth while, at the same time, moving toward the base runner so a tag can take place (which results in the runner being put out). The objective for the base runner is to reach one of the two bases safely without being tagged. One point is awarded to the base runner if successful. After each play, the players should rotate positions so that the previous base runner becomes one of the two fielders.

Hot Potato Softball

Introduction: This three-player softball game recreates the use of a "relay" thrower. The one-minute time limit adds to the excitement of this throwing and catching contest.

Number of Players: 3

Suggested Grade Levels: 2nd–6th grades, two bases

Equipment: 1 whiffle ball, 2 bases

How to Play: The play area consists of a large open area with two bases placed approximately 40-60 feet apart. Designate two players to start on the bases as the fielders, and a third player positioned in the middle of the bases as the "relay" player. One of the fielders begins with the ball.

On a starting signal, the fielder with the ball throws the ball to the player in the middle (the relay player), who quickly turns and throws the ball to the third player. The third player immediately returns the ball to the relay player, who turns and throws the ball to the first thrower. One point is awarded to the relay thrower for each throw to a fielder. The objective is to have as many points possible in one minute. After each one-minute period, the players should rotate positions so that all players have an opportunity to be the relay thrower.

Softball Goalie

Introduction: This two-player game simulates the skill needed to successfully field a ground ball in a softball game. The 30-second time limit adds an additional challenge to the contest.

Number of Players: 2

Suggested Grade Levels: K–8th grades

Equipment: 3–4 whiffle balls, 2 cones

How to Play: The play area consists of an open area with two cones placed approximately 6-8 feet apart. Designate one player to be the fielder and have him or her positioned in the middle of the cones. The other player is the feeder, and he or she stands about 10-12 feet away from the fielder. The feeder starts with one ball in hand and several balls nearby on the ground.

On a starting signal, the player with the ball (the feeder) rolls the ball to the left, right, and directly at the player in the middle (the fielder), attempting to get the ground ball past him or her. The feeder must throw the ball in an underhanded fashion, and it must hit the ground between the two cones and before reaching the fielder. After catching the grounder, the fielder tosses the ball underhanded to the feeder and immediately returns to a ready position to await the next throw. If the ball goes past the fielder, the feeder picks up another ball from his/her side and quickly resumes the game with the new ball. One point is awarded to the feeder for each grounder that gets past the fielder. The feeder's objective is to have as many points possible in the 30-second time limit. After each period, the players rotate positions.

Dueling Pitchers

Introduction: This one-on-one game develops throwing and catching skills.

Number of Players: 2

Suggested Grade Levels: 1st–6th grades

Equipment: 1 whiffle ball, 2 beanbags (or similar objects for marking spots)

How to Play: Have each player work with a partner. The two players stand about six feet apart facing each other. Give each player a beanbag or similar object for marking spots. One player is also given a ball.

The objective is to end the game being the pitcher who was able to throw a "strike" from the furthest distance. The player with the ball starts the game as the first pitcher. His or her partner begins as the catcher. The pitcher throws the ball toward the catcher in such a way that it can be caught without the catcher moving his or her feet (and without the ball hitting the ground before arriving to the catcher). If the catcher moves his or her feet, or if the ball doesn't arrive to the catcher in the air, a "strike" cannot be called (regardless if the catcher successfully catches the ball or not), and the pitcher cannot take a step back. With each successfully thrown strike, the pitcher takes one step back. If the pitcher throws a pitch which is not a strike, he or she places a bean bag at that spot and the players reverse roles. Each player keeps their beanbag at the spot at their furthest thrown strike.

Dueling Batters

Introduction: This one-on-one activity gives players an opportunity to practice directionality and distance when batting. It also provides practice at fielding a batted ball.

Number of Players: 2

Suggested Grade Levels: 3rd–8th grades

Equipment: 1 whiffle ball, 2 batting tees, 4 cones

How to Play: With an open area, set up the two batting tees directly in line with each other about 40-60 feet apart. Place two cones about 15 feet apart on each side of the cones. Designate one student to bat first and the other to field. The designated batter places the ball on his or her tee.

Play begins when the batter hits the ball off the tee, trying to hit the ball past the other player while keeping it within the area defined by the cones (scoring one point). The batter can hit the ball past the fielder (and between the cones) by hitting it on the ground or by hitting a fly ball. The fielding player must catch the ball in front of the cones in order to prevent the batter from scoring. The players alternate between hitting and fielding after each play.

Depending on the age and skill levels, give players the opportunity to adjust the distance and width of the cones if needed.

Softball Darts

Introduction: This lively and competitive activity resembles the indoor game of Darts. It also provides students an opportunity to practice directionality when batting.

Number of Players: 2

Suggested Grade Levels: 2nd–8th grades

Equipment: 3 whiffle balls, 1 batting tee, a softball backstop, 1 large hula hoop, duct tape

How to Play: Set up a batting tee directly in front of a softball backstop about 10-15 feet away. Tie a hula hoop to the middle of the backstop (for the target). Place the ball on the tee and designate one player to bat first.

Play begins when the batter hits the ball off the tee, trying to hit the ball into the hula hoop target (scoring one point). After each swing, the batter places another ball on the tee. After three hit balls, the players switch. Remind the awaiting player not batting to stand at a safe distance from the tee. The objective is to end with the highest point total.

Depending on the age and skill levels, give players the opportunity to adjust the distance and/or size of the target.

Home Run Derby

Introduction: As the name implies, the emphasis of Home Run Derby is to hit the ball as far as possible. Besides batting, other skills developed include catching and pitching.

Number of Players: 4-6

Suggested Grade Levels: 3rd–8th grades

Equipment: 3 whiffle balls, 1 batting tee (if needed), and 3 cones

How to Play: The game is played on a regular softball field. Place a cone on first, second, and third bases (this represents the home run restraining line). The players start in the positions of batter, catcher, pitcher, and two fielders (or three fielders if playing with a group total of six players).

Play begins when the pitcher throws underhand to the batter who attempts to hit the ball beyond the restraining line of cones. The batter can hit the ball past the cones by hitting it on the ground (scoring one point) or by hitting a fly ball (scoring two points). The batter is allowed three pitches to accumulate points. The players in the field serve only as shaggers for the batter. After three pitches, the batter becomes the left fielder, the left fielder moves to center field, center fielder to right field, right fielder to pitcher, pitcher to catcher, and the catcher becomes the new batter.

Depending on their skill levels, give players the opportunity to adjust the distance of the cones if needed.

Home Run Bunts

Introduction: As opposed to Home Run Derby (where the emphasis is on distance), Home Run Bunts is a contest of bunting the ball accurately for points. Besides batting, other skills developed include catching and pitching.

Number of Players: 4-6

Suggested Grade Levels: 3rd–8th grades

Equipment: 3 whiffle balls, 1 whiffle bat, 4 cones

How to Play: The game is played on a regular softball field. Place two cones on both base lines about 3 feet apart and about 8-12 feet from the batter's box. The players start in the positions of batter, catcher, pitcher, and two fielders (or three fielders if playing with a group total of six players).

Play begins when the pitcher throws underhand to the batter who attempts to bunt the ball between the two cones on either the right or left side (near the first and second base lines) for a point. The batter must bunt the ball past the cones by hitting it on the ground. The batter is allowed three pitches to accumulate points. After three pitches, the batter becomes the left fielder, the left fielder moves to center field, center fielder to right field, right fielder to pitcher, pitcher to catcher, and the catcher becomes the new batter. Each player's objective is to end the game with the highest number of points.

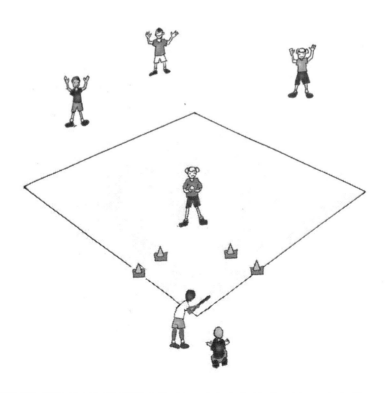

Track & Field Games

Sprint Tag

Introduction: This one-on-one contest enhances the acceleration and speed techniques of sprinting.

Number of Players: 2

Suggested Grade Levels: 3rd–8th grades

Equipment: 1 cone, 1 poly spot

How to Play: Using a large open area, mark off a starting line at one end and place a cone at the other end about 40-60 feet away. Put a poly spot on the ground a few feet in front of the starting line. Position one player behind the starting line, and the other player behind the cone.

The player standing behind the cone begins the game by jogging toward the player on the starting line. Once the jogger touches the poly spot, he or she immediately turns and sprints full speed back toward the cone. Meanwhile, the player that was waiting behind the starting line now chases and attempts to tag the other player before he or she makes back to the cone. The fleeing player is awarded one point if successful. However, the chasing player is awarded a point if he or she tags the fleeing player first. The players switch roles after each race.

Depending on the age and skill levels, give players the opportunity to adjust the distance of the cone from the starting line if needed.

Math Sprints

Introduction: This running game enhances sprinting speed, and integrates movement with math.

Number of Players: 2

Suggested Grade Levels: 3rd–8th grades

Equipment: 2 cones, 1 poly spot

How to Play: Using the two cones, mark off a safety line at each end of the play area. Put a poly spot in the middle of the two safety cones. The players begin by facing each other on opposite sides of the poly spot. Designate one player as "more," and the other as "less."

The two players begin by holding one hand behind their back. Their hand should have up to five fingers hidden from view. On a starting signal, they immediately show their hand. If the sum of both partners' fingers is greater than five, the "more" player turns and sprints full speed back toward the cone. Meanwhile, the other player (the "less" player) now chases and attempts to tag the "more" player before he or she makes back to his or her cone. The "more" player is awarded one point if successful. However, if the sum is five or less, the "less" player runs to his or her cone and the "more" player pursues.

Depending on the age and skill levels, give players the opportunity to adjust the distance of the safety lines. Also, consider having the students try multiplying or subtracting the fingers to come up with a sum amount.

RPS Sprints

Introduction: This fun activity provides the suspense of playing Rock-Paper-Scissors with the excitement of sprinting. It can be played indoors or outdoors.

Number of Players: 2 players

Suggested Grade Levels: 3rd–8th grades

Equipment: 2 cones, 1 poly spot

How to Play: Using the two cones, mark off a safety line at each end of the play area (approximately 60 feet). Put a poly spot in the middle of the two safety cones. The players begin by facing each other on opposite sides of the poly spot.

The game begins with the two players counting to three and performing a rock, paper, scissors. A rock is a closed fist, paper is a flat hand, and scissors are the index and middle fingers in a cutting position. Paper covers rock, rock breaks scissors, and scissors cut paper. The winning player chases the losing player toward his or her safety cone attempting to make a tag. If successful, the chasing player is credited with a point. Only the winner of the rock, Paper, Scissors contest can chase and score points. After each turn, the players return to the middle and play again.

Depending on the age and skill levels, give players the opportunity to adjust the distance of the safety cones.

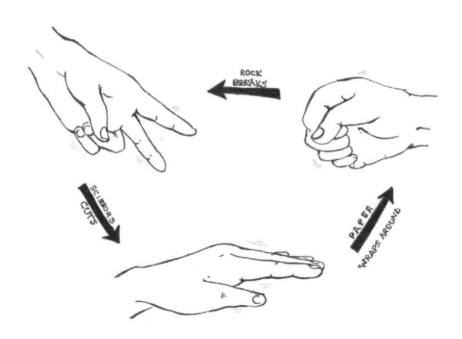

RPS Baton Tag

Introduction: This exciting activity uses a pool noodle for a "baton," and combines a jumping version of Rock-Paper-Scissors with sprinting. It can be played indoors or outdoors.

Number of Players: 2 players

Suggested Grade Levels: 3rd–8th grades

Equipment: 2 cones, 1 half-size noodle

How to Play: Using the two cones, mark off a safety line at each end of the play area (approximately 60 feet). Place a half-size pool noodle (the "baton") on the ground in the middle of the two safety cones. The players begin by facing each other on opposite sides of the pool noodle.

The game begins with the two players counting to three (by jumping with the feet together at the same time) and performing a standing rock, paper, scissors. A rock is landing with both feet together, paper is landing with both feet wide apart, and scissors is landing with the feet split in a forward-backward position. Paper covers rock, rock breaks scissors, and scissors cut paper. The winning player grabs the baton (the noodle) and chases the losing player toward his or her safety cone attempting to make a tag with the noodle. If successful, the chasing player is credited with a point. Only the winner of the rock, Paper, Scissors contest can chase and score points. After each turn, the players return to the middle, place the noodle on the floor, and play again.

Roll & Run

Introduction: This running game can be played indoors or outdoors. It enhances sprinting speed and integrates movement with math challenges.

Number of Players: 2

Suggested Grade Levels: 3rd–8th grades

Equipment: 2 cones, 1 dice, 1 poly spot

How to Play: Using the two cones, mark off a safety line at each end of the play area. Put a poly spot in the middle of the two safety cones. The players begin by facing each other on opposite sides of the poly spot. Designate one player as "Even," and the other as "Odd." Give one player the dice.

The player with the dice begins the game by rolling it on the poly spot. If the dice comes up even, the odd player turns and sprints full speed back toward the cone. Meanwhile, the even player now chases and attempts to tag the odd player before he or she makes back to the cone. The odd player is awarded one point if he or she is successful at avoiding the tag. However, if dice comes up odd, the even player runs to his or her cone and the odd player pursues.

Depending on the age and skill levels, give players the opportunity to adjust the distance of the safety lines. Also, consider having the players try multiplying or subtracting with two dice to come up with a sum amount.

Raceway Sprinting

Introduction: This running game uses a "race track" and enhances sprinting techniques.

Number of Players: 4

Suggested Grade Levels: 3rd–8th grades

Equipment: 4 cones (or a softball infield with 4 bases)

How to Play: Using the four cones, set up an oval-shaped race track with each cone spaced approximately 50-80 feet apart. A softball infield with four bases would also be a great setting for this game. Have one player positioned by each cone or base.

On a starting signal, each player begins the race by running around the track in a clockwise direction, touching each cone or base. The goal is for players to sprint as fast as possible and tag the player in front of them, who also is attempting to tag the next player. The race continues until one player has eventually tagged a player ahead of him or her. After each contest, the players line up again at their starting cone and begin a new race in the opposite direction.

Frisbee Cross Country

Introduction: Frisbee Cross Country improves cardiovascular endurance by combining distance running with frisbee tossing.

Number of Players: 2

Suggested Grade Levels: 3rd–8th grades

Equipment: 4 cones, 2 frisbees

How to Play: Using a large open area and the cones, mark off a cross country course. Instead of cones, another alternative for measuring a course would be to use objects such as trees, baseball backstops, soccer goals, and so forth. For younger children, the distance can be a quarter mile or less. For older children, the distance can be a half mile or longer. Distribute one frisbee to each player, and have both players stand on the starting line.

On a starting signal, each player tosses his or her frisbee as far as possible along the course, runs to pick it up, and throws it again. The players continue in this fashion, running and throwing as fast as possible, until each has covered the course and returned to the starting line. The objective is to cover the distance in as few throws as possible and/or be the first back.

Pony Express Relay

Introduction: This baton-exchange game builds cardiovascular endurance in a challenging and fun setting.

Number of Players: 4 to a team

Suggested Grade Levels: 3rd–8th grades

Equipment: 4 cones, 1 baton for each team, 1 stopwatch (if needed)

How to Play: Using a large open area and the cones, design an oval shape course. The four cones should be equally spaced apart. Form a team of four players, and assign each of the players to stand by a cone. The player at cone #1 begins with a baton and stopwatch in hand.

On a starting signal, the runner at cone #1 carries the baton to the teammate at cone #2. After handing off the baton, the runner from cone #1 stays at cone #2. The runner from cone #2 carries the baton to the teammate at cone #3, hands off the baton, and stays there. The runner from cone #3 carries the baton to cone #4, hands off the baton, and stays there. The runner from cone #4 has to carry the baton all the way past cone #1 (which as no teammate) to the next teammate who is waiting at cone #2. With every race, the runner at cone #4 will have to run "double duty." Play continues in this fashion until all of the runners are back in their original starting positions. Runner #1 also stops the timing with the stopwatch as soon as he or she arrives back. The objective is to continuously have faster times with each race. With a large group, have multiple teams of four players compete against each other at the same time.

Arm Sprints

Introduction: Wheelbarrow racing adds a different twist to "sprinting." Basically, this is simply arm sprinting with a partner holding the legs of a human wheelbarrow. Although it can be exhausting, this activity is always a barrel of laughs for everyone involved.

Number of Players: 4

Suggested Grade Levels: K–8th grades

Equipment: 2 cones

How to Play: Using a grassy area that is flat and smooth, place two cones about 30-50 feet apart for the starting and finishing lines. Form two teams of two players each. One player from each team begins as the "wheelbarrow" on the starting line, while the partner holds his or her legs.

On a starting signal, the two human wheelbarrows "sprint" to the finishing line. The wheelbarrow players attempt to move their arms as fast as possible without collapsing or having their partner drop their legs. At any time, the players can switch positions. It's important to emphasize the need for switching as any one player's strength or weakness can vary considerably. The objective is to be the first team to the finish line.

Cross Country ABC's

Introduction: Cross Country ABC's integrates academics with cross country running. Besides enhancing cardiovascular fitness, children practice spelling and letter identification.

Number of Players: 2

Suggested Grade Levels: 2nd–6th grades

Equipment: Cones (or playground objects for marking), 1 shortened (3" or less) pencil, 1 alphabet tally sheet

How to Play: Using a large open area and the cones, mark off a cross country course. Instead of cones, another alternative for measuring a course would be to use objects such as trees, baseball backstops, soccer goals, and so forth. For younger children, the distance can be a quarter mile or less. For older children, the distance can be a half mile or longer. Distribute one shortened pencil and tally sheet to each pair. Other than recording, the pencil cannot be held and must stay in the back pocket. Have both players stand on the starting line.

Have the players begin by jogging around the course. At the same time, they are work together to observe their surroundings in order to identify at least one item outside that starts with each letter of the alphabet. This can be a playground object, a person's name, an animal, and so forth. For safety purposes, the players must come to a stop to record the word onto their tally sheet. However, when finished, they should immediately start jogging again. The objective is to finish the course and have the tally sheet filled in with words that represent each letter of the alphabet.

Hula Hoop Triple Jumping

Introduction: This fun event uses hula hoops to create a "triple jumping" experience for children.

Number of Players: 2

Suggested Grade Levels: K–6th grades

Equipment: 4 hula hoops, 2 small cones, 2 medium cones, 2 large cones

How to Play: Using an open area, place the four hoops in a straight line. Each hoop should be supported on opposite sides by cones that are paired according to height. The first hoop lays flat on the floor and each succeeding hoop is progressively raised higher. The hoops should a few feet apart. Assign two players to a jumping "pit."

In turn, the players begin at the lowest level and progress as far as possible without dislodging a hoop. When a height is missed the player replaces the hoop on the cones and returns to the beginning. Encourage the players to use a standing jump with a two-foot takeoff and landing, and to use their arms.

For older players, consider creating higher jumping levels by selecting support objects that are higher than the cones. This can be cardboard boxes, benches, trash cans, and so forth.

Javel-Noodle Throw

Introduction: This easy and fun activity requires throwing a pool noodle instead of a javelin.

Number of Players: 2

Suggested Grade Levels: K–6th grades

Equipment: 2 cones, 1 noodle, 2 beanbags (or similar object for marking)

How to Play: Using an open area, place two cones about 6 feet apart for the throwing restraining line. Each player is given a beanbag for distance marking and a noodle (the "javelin").

One player starts by running toward the restraining line and tossing the noodle as far as possible with the same technique as in the javelin event. A foul is called if the player passes the restraining line before releasing the noodle. After the toss, the player places a beanbag at the spot where the noodle hit. The next player tosses his or her noodle and records the distance with a beanbag. Both players take turns attempting to throw further with each toss.

Discus Frisbee

Introduction: This unique activity creates a simulation of the discus event. This is accomplished by taking two frisbees and taping them back to back to make one solid discus.

Number of Players: 2

Suggested Grade Levels: K–8th grades

Equipment: 2 cones, 4 frisbees (2 taped back-to-back to make a discus), 2 beanbags (or similar object for marking)

How to Play: Using an open area, place two cones about 6 feet apart for the throwing restraining line. Each player is given a frisbee discus (two frisbees taped back to back) and a beanbag for marking distances.

One player starts by spinning toward the restraining line and tossing the frisbee discus as far as possible with the same technique as in the discus event. A foul is called if the player passes the restraining line before releasing the discus. After the toss, the player places a beanbag at the spot where the discus hit. The next player tosses his or her discus and records the distance with a beanbag. Both players take turns attempting to throw further with each toss.

Noodle High Jumping

Introduction: This is a simulation of the high jump event with the use of a pool noodle.

Number of Players: 3

Suggested Grade Levels: 2nd–8th grades

Equipment: 1 pool noodle

How to Play: Using an open area, have two players hold up the pool noodle for the high jump "bar." A third player is positioned about 15 feet to be the first jumper.

The first jumper approaches the pool noodle (being held by the two teammates at knee height) and jumps over the pool noodle. A player has two chances to clear the "bar." The two noodle holders are not to grab the ends—rather, they are let the noodle ends rest in the palms of their hands. This way, the noodle will fall easily if contact is made. In turn the other players jump over the noodle at the same knee-high height. After each player has jumped that height, the noodle holders raise it to the waist, getting progressively higher.

Indoor Triathlon Duel

Introduction: These three indoor triathlon events (running, rolling a hoop, and scooter "swimming") develop strength, aerobic fitness, and provides lots of fun.

Number of Players: 2

Suggested Grade Levels: 3rd–8th grades

Equipment: 2 cones, 2 hula hoops, 2 scooters

How to Play: Using a gymnasium, design a triathlon course with the cones and divide it into three activity zones. The three zones will require players to run, run while rolling a hula hoop, and perform a scooter "swim." Have each player partner with another. Each player will have a hula hoop positioned at the start of the second section of the race, and a scooter at the third section.

On a signal, the two players run as fast as possible to the second section, where they pick up a hula hoop and roll it continuously while moving toward the third section. At the third section, each player lies down on a scooter and pretends to swim all the way to the finish line. The objective is to finish the course (all three events) as quickly as possible.

Outdoor Triathlon Duel

Introduction: Improved cardiovascular endurance is the primary benefit of this exciting activity that includes several outdoor triathlon events.

Number of Players: 2

Suggested Grade Levels: 3rd–8th grades

Equipment: 2 cones, 2 tennis balls, 2 jump ropes

How to Play: Using an open area with the cones, design a triathlon course and divide it into three activity zones. The three zones will require players to run, run while self-tossing a tennis ball, and jump rope while running. Have each player partner with another. Each player will have a short jump rope positioned at the start of the second section of the race, and a tennis ball at the third section.

On a signal, the two players run as fast as possible to the second section, where they turn a jump rope and run at the same time to the third section. At the third section, each player picks up a tennis ball and self-tosses it a few feet in the air while running and catching it all the way to the finish line. The objective is to finish the course (all three events) as quickly as possible.

Scooter Sports

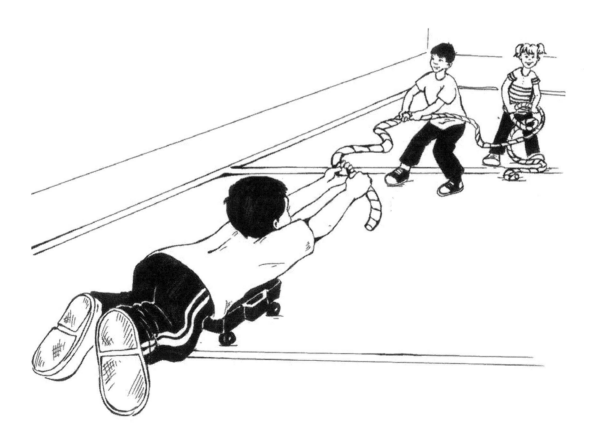

Scooter Hockey Duel

Introduction: This one-on-one game utilizes the short hockey sticks and scooters available in most physical education catalogs. It maximizes stick handling opportunities and requires tremendous hustle and energy.

Number of Players: 2

Suggested Grade Levels: 3rd–8th grades

Equipment: 1 short hockey stick and scooter for each player, 1 puck, 2 cones

How to Play: The play area consists of two cones placed approximately 15-20 feet apart. There are no boundary lines. The two players start in the middle of the two cones, seated on scooters, with each facing the cone that they will attempt to hit with the puck.

The game begins with a "face-off" (a series of three taps with the sticks before hitting the puck) in the middle of the two cones. The objective is to control the puck and scoot toward the opponent's cone in order to shoot and hit it for a score. If successful, one point is scored and the puck is placed back in the middle for another face-off. A player may attempt to steal the puck at any time to become the offensive player. Since there are boundary lines, players can shoot and hit an opponent's cone from any angle.

No player can touch the puck with his or her hands, and no physical contact (including high-sticking) is allowed. A violation results in the other player gaining possession at the spot of the infraction.

Scooter Hockey Doubles

Introduction: As the name implies, Scooter Hockey Doubles is a two-on-two game. This natural progression of Scooter Hockey Duel (one-on-one floor hockey) maximizes stick handling opportunities with lots of scooter movement.

Number of Players: 4

Suggested Grade Levels: 3rd–8th grades

Equipment: 1 short hockey stick and scooter for each player, 1 puck, 2 pylon cones

How to Play: The play area consists of two cones placed about 20 feet apart. There are no boundary lines. Form two teams of two players each. Each player begins with a short hockey stick and scooter. There are no designated positions, except playing the goalie position should be limited (instead, passing and offensive teamwork should be encouraged).

This game is played much like Scooter Hockey Duel (page 128) except now there are two players on each team and the skill of passing is utilized. Two opposing players, seated on scooters, start with a face-off in the middle of the play area. The objective is to control the puck and drive toward the opponent's cone in order to shoot and hit the cone for a score. If successful, one point is scored and the puck is brought back to the middle for another face-off. Defensive players may attempt to steal the puck at any time to gain possession. Since there are no boundary lines, players can shoot and hit an opponent's cone from any angle. Rough play, including high-sticking, is not allowed. A violation results in the other team gaining possession of the puck at the spot of the infraction.

Scooter Mini Hockey

Introduction: This three-on-three activity is a natural progression of Scooter Hockey Duel (one-on-one hockey) and Scooter Hockey Doubles (two-on-two hockey). It maximizes stick handling opportunities, and enhances many of the major skills of playing floor hockey while using scooter movements.

Number of Players: 6

Suggested Grade Levels: 4th–8th grades

Equipment: 1 short hockey stick and scooter for each player, 1 puck, 4 cones

How to Play: The play area consists of two goals about 20-30 feet apart. For goals, place two cones about 5 feet apart. There are no boundary lines. Form two teams of three players each. Designate two forwards and one goalie on each team. All players begin with a short hockey stick and scooter.

This game is played much like Scooter Hockey Doubles *except* now there are three players on each team and the position of goalie is introduced. Two opposing players, seated on scooters, start with a face-off in the middle of the play area. The objective is to control the puck and drive toward the opponent's goal in order to shoot and hit the puck through the two cones for a score. If successful, one point is scored and the puck is brought back to the middle for another face-off. Defensive players may attempt to steal the puck at any time to gain possession. Since there are no boundary lines, players can score from any angle (including backwards through the two cones). Have teammates rotate positions throughout the game.

Rough play, including high-sticking, is not allowed. A violation results in the other team gaining possession of the puck at the spot of the infraction.

Scooter Swimming

Introduction: This activity simulates the arm movement skills associated with swimming. It also develops upper body strength, agility, and coordination.

Number of Players: 2

Suggested Grade Levels: K-6th grades

Equipment: 1 scooter for each player

How to Play: Hand each player a scooter, and have them pair up. Using the floor and walls of a gymnasium (the "swimming pool"), have the players first practice various swim strokes with their arms while positioned on a scooter. This includes the crawl stroke, back stroke, breast stroke, and so forth. Also, introduce the "turtle turn" and have the players practice turning on their scooters and pushing off the wall with their feet.

After the players have mastered the above skills, consider having a "swim meet" duel. Basically, it would look much like a one-on-one swim meet. Swimming lanes can be marked off using floor tape or cones, and the gym wall can be used for executing the turtle turns.

Have fun swimming!

Scooter Tug-o-War

Introduction: Here's a fun twist to having a tug-o-war contest!

Number of Players: 4–6

Suggested Grade Levels: 2nd–8th grades

Equipment: 1 scooter for each player, 1 tug-o-war rope, 2 cones

How to Play: Hand each player a scooter, and form two equal teams of 2-3 players. Place the tug-o-war rope (about 12 feet in length) on the floor. Position a cone about two feet away on each side of the center mark. Both teams begin by stationing themselves on their side of the rope. All players must be seated and their feet on the floor. Players will have more space and better balance by alternating sides of the rope when positioning for the contest.

On a signal, both teams start pulling. The contest ends when one of the teams pulls the center of the rope to their cone. Have the teams play several times with players in different positions each time.

As a safety precaution, remind the players to never let go of the rope. Also, players should quickly get back on their scooters if they fall off.

Scooter Mountaineering

Introduction: Here's a fun activity to practice rope traversing while using a scooter. Besides building upper body strength, the skills of using teamwork and cooperation are also enhanced.

Number of Players: 3

Suggested Grade Levels: 3rd–8th grades

Equipment: 1 scooter for each group, 1 rope (20 feet or longer)

How to Play: Group the students into threes. Each group should have one rope and one scooter. Place a rope (minimum of 20 feet) on the floor in a straight line. For older students, the rope should be as long as possible from one wall to another. Two players grip the ends of the rope in a sitting or kneeling position. The third player places the scooter over the rope at one end, and grabs the rope with his or her hands.

The player on the scooter begins by pulling himself or herself (with the hands only) to the other end of the rope. When done, the player changes place with that rope holder who now crosses the rope. Play continues in this fashion with each player having several turns.

Variations: For an added challenge, have the traversing player lie on his/her back while on the scooter.

Scooter Fencing

Introduction: This one-on-one game is a modification of the sport of fencing, and is a great energizer!

Number of Players: 2

Suggested Grade Levels: 3rd-8th grades

Equipment: 1 pool noodle and scooter for each player

How to Play: Arrange the students into pairs. The two players start with a noodle in hand and seated on scooters.

Using the pool noodle, the objective is to make contact with one of the opponent's feet for a score (worth one point), while at the same time, avoid having the feet hit by the opponent. Players can move around (while seated on the scooter), pick up their feet, and use their noodles to avoid contact. Play continues in this fashion for a predetermined number of points or time.

During play, remind the players they are to remain seated on their scooter and are not allowed to leave their scooter. Additionally, players cannot swing their noodles above the opponent's foot level.

Scooter Polo

Introduction: This unique game simulates the sport of Polo in that the riding on scooters represents horseback riding.

Number of Players: 4–6

Suggested Grade Levels: 3rd–8th grades

Equipment: 1 noodle and scooter for each player, 1 whiffle ball, 4 cones

How to Play: Arrange the players into two equal teams of two or three players each. The players start with a noodle in hand and seated on scooters. Place two cones (for goals) at opposite ends of the play area. The whiffle ball is set in the middle of the play area. There are no boundary lines.

On a signal, the players scoot to reach the whiffle ball and attempt to advance the ball toward their goal for a score. One point is scored when the ball passes through the opponent's two cones. Since there are no boundary lines, a score can be made from either side of the cones. Passes and shots can only be made with the noodle (that is, players cannot advance the ball or make a shot with their feet or hands). Play continues in this fashion for a predetermined number of points or time.

Players are to remain seated on their scooter and are not allowed to leave their scooter. Additionally, players cannot swing their noodles above the opponent's foot level.

Scooter Lacrosse

Introduction: The use of plastic scoops and a plastic ball allow students to develop throwing and catching skills similar to those used in lacrosse.

Number of Players: 4–6

Suggested Grade Levels: 4th–8th grades

Equipment: 1 plastic scoop and scooter for each player, 1 whiffle ball, 2 basketball backboards (or substitute a wall target)

How to Play: Arrange the players into two equal teams of two or three players each. The players start with a plastic scoop in hand and seated on scooters. Designate basketball backboards or two wall targets (for the goals) at opposite ends of the play area. There are no boundary lines. One team is designated to start with the whiffle ball in the middle of the play area.

On a signal, the designated player on the beginning offensive team starts the game by passing the ball with his or her scoop to a teammate. The offensive team tries to move the ball toward the opponent's backboard by throwing and catching with the scoops, and attempts to score by throwing and hitting the backboard (worth one point). The offensive player in possession of the ball is allowed to move on his/her scooter, but has only five seconds to pass or shoot. Any player who violates the five seconds rule forfeits the ball to the opponents at that spot. Passes and shots can only be made with the scoop (that is, players cannot advance the ball or make a shot with their feet or hands). The defensive team can intercept or scoop up a loose ball at any time. After each score, the non-scoring team starts play again by passing the ball in from behind the backboard (as in basketball). Play continues in this fashion for a predetermined number of points or time.

Scooter Handball

Introduction: This fun game introduces children to the strategy and skills of handball throwing and catching.

Number of Players: 6

Suggested Grade Levels: 4th–8th grades

Equipment: 1 scooter for each player, 1 foam ball, 2 folding tumbling mats

How to Play: Set a tumbling mat upright at each end of the play area for the two goals. There are no boundary lines. Arrange the players into two equal teams of three players each. The players start on their half of the play area and seated on scooters. Each team has one goalie and two forwards. One team is designated to start with the ball on offense.

On a signal, the designated player on the beginning offensive team starts the game by passing the ball to a teammate. The offensive team tries to move the ball toward the opponent's backboard by throwing and catching, and attempts to score by throwing and hitting the mat (worth one point). The offensive player in possession of the ball is not allowed to move on his/her scooter, and has only five seconds to pass or shoot. Any player who violates the five seconds rule forfeits the ball to the opponents at that spot. The defensive team can intercept or pick up a dropped ball at any time, but they are not allowed to steal the ball from the hands of an offensive player. All players must remain seated on their scooters and are not allowed to leave their scooters. After each score, the non-scoring team starts play again by passing the ball at the mid-court area.

Scooter Football

Introduction: This "indoor arena" version of football develops passing and receiving skills—and, requires plenty of cooperation and teamwork.

Number of Players: 6

Suggested Grade Levels: 4th–8th grades

Equipment: 1 scooter for each player, 1 foam football, 4 cones

How to Play: Place two cones about 10-12 feet apart at each end of the play area for the goal lines. There are no boundary lines. Arrange the players into two equal teams of three players each. The players start on their designated half of the play area and are seated on scooters. One team is designated to start with the ball on offense. Designate one player as the quarterback and the other two as receivers.

The object of the game is to score a touchdown by crossing the opponent's goal line with the football while seated on a scooter. Since there are no kickoffs, the offensive team begins play in the middle of the play area with the quarterback holding the football. The two receivers line up next to the quarterback facing the opponents. The defensive team must start at least 5 yards away from the offensive players. On "Hike," the receivers scoot down the court to catch a pass from the quarterback. If completed, the receiver with possession of the ball can scoot forward toward the opponent's goal until tagged with two hands by a defensive player. This counts as a tackle and the play ends at that spot. If the ball is dropped or hits the ground at any time during play, the play is also over and counts as a down. After each play, the three offensive players line up in the same positions as before and play continues. The offensive team has up to four downs to score. If the offensive team does not score after the fourth down, the ball goes over to the other team at midfield and they now have up to four downs to score going in the opposite direction. Also, after a touchdown, the non-scoring team starts with the ball at midfield. All players must remain on their scooters (seated or on knees) and are not allowed to leave their scooters.

Scooter Basketball

Introduction: Scooter Basketball is a challenging variation on the regular game of basketball, and develops the skills of passing, catching, and shooting.

Number of Players: 6

Suggested Grade Levels: 4th–8th grades

Equipment: 1 scooter for each player, 1 basketball, 4 tumbling mats

How to Play: Place two tumbling mats at each end of the play area. The mats are to be set upright in an open, square formation. Arrange the players into two equal teams of three players each. The players start at midcourt on their scooters. Designate one team to start on offense.

On a signal, the beginning offensive team starts the game by passing the ball to a teammate. The offensive team tries to move the ball toward the opponent's backboard by throwing and catching, and attempts to score by shooting the basketball into the square. The offensive player in possession of the ball is allowed to move on his/her scooter, but has only five seconds to pass or shoot. Any player who violates the five seconds rule forfeits the ball to the opponents at that spot. This is strictly a passing and catching game, and dribbling is not allowed. The defensive team can intercept a pass, block a shot, or pick up a loose ball at any time. However, they are not allowed to steal the ball from the hands of an offensive player, nor can they make contact of any type. After each score, the non-scoring team starts play again by passing the ball inbounds from beside the mats. The players are to remain on their scooter (seated on their bottoms or on their knees) at all times during play.

Scooter Rugby

Introduction: This fun game is a non-contact modification of rugby. It develops throwing and catching skills, and requires plenty of teamwork.

Number of Players: 6

Suggested Grade Levels: 4th–8th grades

Equipment: 1 scooter for each player, 1 rugby ball (or substitute a football), 4 cones

How to Play: Place two cones about 8-10 feet apart at each end of the play area for the goals. There are no boundary lines. Arrange the players into two equal teams of three players each. The teams start on their designated half of the play area and the players are seated on scooters. Designate one team to start with the ball on offense.

The object of the game is to score a touchdown by placing the ball on the floor past the opponent's goal. Play begins at midfield with one of the two offensive linemen (who are seated on their scooters with shoulders touching) throwing the ball backwards in an underhanded motion to the running back. The defensive team must start at least 5 yards away from the offensive linemen. The running back can scoot forward on his or scooter, or pass the ball backwards anytime to a teammate. The offensive player with possession of the ball can scoot forward toward the opponent's goal until tagged with two hands by a defensive player. This counts as a tackle and the play ends at that spot. If the ball is dropped or hits the ground at any time during play, the play is also over and counts as a down. After each play, the three offensive players line up in the same positions as before and play continues. The offensive team has up to six downs to score. If the offensive team does not score after the sixth down, the ball goes over to the other team at the spot of the last touch and they now have up to six downs to score going in the opposite direction. All players must remain seated on their scooters and are not allowed to leave their scooters.

Partner Gymnastics

Partner Stand-Ups

Introduction: This fun activity calls for balance, strength, and lots of cooperation!

Number of Players: 2

Suggested Grade Levels: K–6th grades

Equipment: 1 tumbling mat

How to Play: Partners sit on the mat facing each other, holding hands and touching toes (feet are flat on the mat). The knees should be bent.

Working together, both players try to stand up simultaneously without releasing their hands. They can only stand up by cooperatively pulling at the same time, and cannot roll over onto their knees.

Have the players repeat several times.

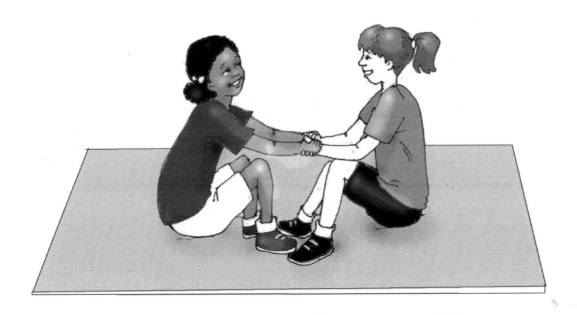

Back Stand-Ups

Introduction: Here's a fun activity for developing leg strength and the skill of cooperation.

Number of Players: 2

Suggested Grade Levels: 2nd–8th grades

Equipment: 1 tumbling mat

How to Play: Both partners sit on the mat with backs together and feet in opposite directions. Their elbows should be hooked and their knees are bent so that their feet are close to their bodies.

Working together, both students try to stand up without releasing their elbows or touching their hands to the floor. They can only stand up by pushing against each other's back.

Variation: Have the partners try standing up without hooking elbows and without using hands. This will definitely challenge your students!

Teeter-Totters

Introduction: This fun activity is for the younger players and it requires body control, strength, and co-operation.

Number of Players: 2

Suggested Grade Levels: K–4ᵗʰ grades

Equipment: 1 tumbling mat

How to Play: Partners are facing each other with knees bent, and each is sitting gently on the other's feet. They should be holding on to each other by grasping each other's upper arm area.

Working together, both players try to rock back and forth (like a "teeter-totter") without releasing their hands. They raise their feet as the partner rises from the floor, and they must keep their feet under the other's seat at all times.

Have the players repeat several times.

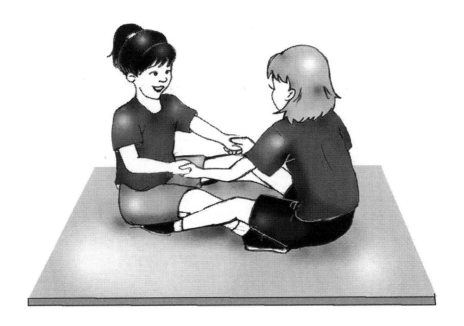

Partner Toe Touches

Introduction: This cooperative activity builds abdominal strength.

Number of Players: 2

Suggested Grade Levels: K–6th grades

Equipment: 1 tumbling mat

How to Play: For best results, instructors should pair the players by height. Partners lie on their backs with heads near each other and feet in opposite directions. Their hands should be joined with a hand-wrist grip.

Working together, both players bring the legs up so that the toes touch directly high above. Both players should strive to stay high up on their shoulder area, and should maintain a steady cadence.

Partner Twister

Introduction: Partner Twister is a fun energizer for a gymnastics unit that will test everyone's balance and flexibility.

Number of Players: 2

Suggested Grade Levels: K–6th grades

Equipment: 1 tumbling mat

How to Play: To begin, partners face each other and grasp right hands loosely so that the hands can turn while touching. One player steps over the arms with the left leg to face the opposite direction (straddling the arms), and continues all the way around to the original face-to-face position without letting go of the right hands. A 360 degree circle has been accomplished without letting of the hands! When finished, players switch roles and repeat.

To avoid getting accidentally kicked, remind players to duck or bend down as the other player is swinging his or her leg over the arms.

Double Bear Balance

Introduction: This is a simple partner balance that the younger players will find challenging and fun.

Number of Players: 2

Suggested Grade Levels: K–4th grades

Equipment: 1 tumbling mat

How to Play: For best results, the instructor should pair players by size. The bottom partner gets down on the hands and knees, and keeps the body as level as possible. The hands should be spread about shoulder width apart.

The top partner assumes the same position directly above the support partner, with the hands on the shoulders and knees on the hips. The final part is to have the top partner pose with his or her eyes up and back straight. As a reminder, the top partner should always avoid stepping on the support partner's lower back area.

Leaping Frogs

Introduction: Leapfrog is a traditional physical education activity that has maintained its place as a desired favorite among children. Despite its name, this is actually a jump and vault movement pattern.

Number of Players: 2

Suggested Grade Levels: K–6th grades

Equipment: 1 tumbling mat

How to Play: The objective is for partners to alternately jump over each from one end of the mat to other end. One partner forms a low back by crouching down on the knees, and curling into a tight ball. The leaper starts a few feet behind the crouched partner.

The leaper begins with a running or fast walking start, puts the hands on the tucked partner at the back at the shoulders, vaults over the partner, and lands on both feet. At the height of the jump, the upper torso should be held erect to avoid a forward fall. The landing should be done with good control, and with a bent-knee action. After the leaper has finished, the players immediately switch roles with the previous leaper now going down into a tucked position.

Wring the Dishrag

Introduction: This partner gymnastics movement requires lots of cooperation. It is also a terrific class energizer and can serve as a prelude to some dance movements.

Number of Players: 2

Suggested Grade Levels: K—6th grades

Equipment: 1 tumbling mat

How to Play: For best results, instructors should pair the players by height. The partners begin by facing each other, raising both arms to the sides, and joining hands. They then take one side (right for one and left for the other) and turn under the arms going back-to-back, and continuing a full turn until back to the original position. After several times, the players reverse directions.

Horizontal Balance

Introduction: This simple balance is a great introductory activity to gymnastics.

Number of Players: 2

Suggested Grade Levels: K–4th grades

Equipment: 1 tumbling mat

How to Play: For best results, the instructor should pair players by size. The bottom support partner lies on the back, arms stretched forward, and knees bent.

The top partner takes a position standing by the support partner's head and facing the support partner's feet. Next, the support partner grasps the top partner by the knees, and the top partner puts his or her hands on the support partner's knees. The support partner then lifts the top partner by the knees until his or her arms are fully extended. The top partner keeps the body straight and the arms fully extended. The top partner should hold this pose for a few seconds. When finished, have the partners switch roles.

Hitchhiking Tandem

Introduction: This is a simple cooperative activity that children of every age will enjoy.

Number of Players: 2

Suggested Grade Levels: K–6th grades

Equipment: 1 tumbling mat

How to Play: For best results, the instructor should pair players by size. The partners begin at one end of the mat, facing each other, and hands on each other's shoulders. One player then gently stands on the other partner's instep area (the mat helps to cushion any pressure there might be). It's also best to have the players take off their shoes.

The objective is to go to the end of the mat and back by walking together and without losing contact with each other. Movement should be under good control, and neither partner should go too fast. When finished, have the partners change roles and repeat.

Partner Sit Balance

Introduction: Here is a fantastic cooperative activity for improving leg strength.

Number of Players: 2

Suggested Grade Levels: 1st–8th grades

Equipment: 1 tumbling mat

How to Play: For best results, the instructor should pair players by size and strength. The partners begin by standing back-to-back with the arms extending straight out.

Working together, the partners keep their backs firmly touching while going down into a sitting position. After the thighs are horizontal to the floor, the partners hold the sitting position for at least five seconds before coming back up. The key to success is pushing against each other's back for support, and moving slowly.

Handshake Rescues

Introduction: Balance, strength, and cooperation are improved by this partner challenge.

Number of Players: 2

Suggested Grade Levels: 3rd–8th grades

Equipment: 1 tumbling mat

How to Play: For best results, the instructor should pair players according to size and strength. Partners crouch down on the mat facing each other, holding right hands, and leaning slightly backward.

Before beginning, partners should be leaning backward to the point that each would fall backward if not holding hands. On a count of three, both partners quickly let go of their right hands and try to catch each other's left hands before completely falling backward.

Have the players repeat several times with different hands.

Ball Stand-Ups

Introduction: A fantastic partner activity for practicing the concept of cooperation.

Number of Players: 2

Suggested Grade Levels: 2nd–8th grades

Equipment: 1 tumbling mat, 1 playground ball (slightly deflated)

How to Play: Both partners sit on the mat with backs together and feet in opposite directions. They then place a playground ball between their upper back areas. A slightly deflated ball works best.

Working together, both players try to stand up while keeping the ball positioned between the backs. To keep the ball from falling, partners should go slow, steady, and be communicating at the same time.

Other body areas where partners can try squeezing the ball and standing up together includes going forehead to forehead and shoulder to shoulder. Partners can also walk down the mat while performing a ball squeeze.

Beach Ball Push-Ups

Introduction: This activity is a favorite of my students. It calls for lots of cooperation, focus, and endurance.

Number of Players: 2

Suggested Grade Levels: 2nd–8th grades

Equipment: 1 tumbling mat, 1 beach ball (8 inch diameter)

How to Play: Both partners lie face down on the mat with heads together and feet in opposite directions. They hold a small beach ball between their heads. A slightly deflated ball works best.

Working together, both players try to up and down with a push-up while keeping the ball positioned between the heads. To keep the ball from falling, partners should go slow, steady, and be communicating at the same time. With each successful push-up, the pair calls out the letters of the alphabet. The objective is to get to the letter "Z" as quickly as possible (or as far along the alphabet as possible). An alternative way of keeping score of push-ups would be to simply do many as possible in a set amount of time.

Basketball Crunches

Introduction: This multi-task activity develops abdominal strength, endurance, cooperation, and catching skills.

Number of Players: 2

Suggested Grade Levels: 3rd–8th grades

Equipment: 1 tumbling mat, 1 basketball

How to Play: Partners face each other about 4-6 feet apart, knees bent, and feet flat on the floor. The partner with the ball starts by lying flat on his/her back and holding the ball with both hands over the top of the head. The partner without the ball is sitting up and waiting to catch the pass.

To begin, the partner with the ball sits up and makes an overhead pass to the awaiting partner. This partner, upon receiving the pass, goes backward to the down position of a crunch and touches the ball to the floor behind and over the top of his/her head. The partners continue the back and forth catching of the ball and performing a crunch-like abdominal exercise. With each successful crunch and catch, the pair calls out the letters of the alphabet. The objective is to get to the letter "Z" as quickly as possible (or as far along the alphabet as possible). An alternative way of keeping score of crunches would be to simply do many as possible in a set amount of time.

Bicycle Tandem

Introduction: Performing the Bicycle Tandem is so much fun—your players won't even know it's an abdominal strength-building activity unless you tell them!

Number of Players: 2

Suggested Grade Levels: K–6th grades

Equipment: 1 tumbling mat

How to Play: For best results, instructors should pair the players by height. Partners sit facing each other with the soles of the feet touching. Both players should be leaning back on their hands for support, and the legs need to be off the mat.

Working together, both players move their legs in a pedaling action. Both players should strive to maintain constant foot contact with a steady cadence. After a while, challenge the partners to reverse their direction. They can also be challenged to go faster and faster.

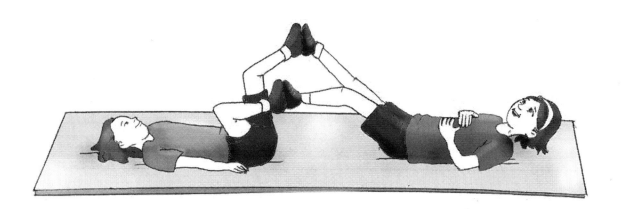

Partner Hopping

Introduction: Players work cooperatively as they attempt to hop and keep balance.

Number of Players: 2

Suggested Grade Levels: K–6th grades

Equipment: 1 tumbling mat

How to Play: The objective is for partners to perform a joint hopping movement from one of the mat to other end. There are two combinations to be tried.

The first challenge requires both partners to face each other a few feet apart. They then extend their right legs forward to be grasped at the ankle by the partner's left hand. They then hold right hands and start hopping on the left leg. When finished, switch leg and hand positions and repeat.

The second challenge calls for the partners to stand side by side with the inside arms around each other's waist. They then lift the inside legs from the floor and start hopping on their outside feet. This is similar to the classic three-legged race, but the legs are not tied together.

For safety purposes, inform the players to immediately release their partner's leg if he or she begins to fall.

Wheelbarrow Partners

Introduction: Performing a wheelbarrow is one of my student's favorite gymnastics activities. The building of upper body strength is the primary benefit (and having fun!).

Number of Players: 2

Suggested Grade Levels: K–6th grades

Equipment: 1 tumbling mat

How to Play: One partner goes down into a push-up position. The other partner grasps the front player's legs about halfway between the ankles and the knees, and lifts the legs to the waist area. The wheelbarrow walks forward with the front player walking on his or her hands. The objective is to go to the end of the mat and back. Movement should be under good control, and the back player should not push too fast. Change roles after each trip.

Partner Leg Balance

Introduction: This is a unique partner balance that is excellent for developing strength of the upper body.

Number of Players: 2

Suggested Grade Levels: 2nd–6th grades

Equipment: 1 tumbling mat

How to Play: For best results, the instructor should pair players by size. The bottom support partner lies on the back, arms stretched upward, and knees bent.

The top partner takes a position standing backwards near the support partner's head, facing forward, and with the legs crossed at the ankles. Next, the support partner grasps the top partner by the ankles, and the top partner puts his or her hands on the floor. The support partner then lifts the top partner by the ankles until the arms are fully extended. The top partner keeps the body straight and the arms fully extended. The crossed ankles of the top partner make it a single leg balance. The top partner should hold this pose for a few seconds. When finished, have the partners switch roles.

Sky Balance

Introduction: This enjoyable activity builds trust, cooperation, balance, and strength.

Number of Players: 2

Suggested Grade Levels: K–6th grades

Equipment: 1 tumbling mat

How to Play: For best results, the instructor should pair players by size. The bottom (support) partner lies on the back, arms outstretched forward, and hands on the thighs. The support partner then raises the legs and positions the soles of the feet facing upward.

The top partner takes a position facing the support partner, grasping his or her hands. The top partner then bends over with the support partner with the support's feet position on the lower abdominal area. The support partner then raises the top partner from the floor by extending the knees. The top partner arches the back, releases the grip, and puts his or arms out to the sides in a flying position. The top partner should this pose for a few seconds. When finished, have the partners switch roles.

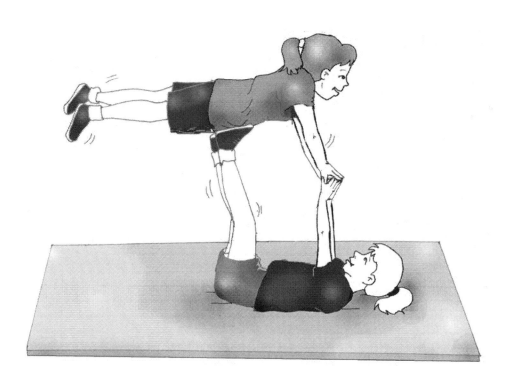

Partner Shoulder Presses

Introduction: Here is a strength builder for children that's also a great cooperative learning activity.

Number of Players: 2

Suggested Grade Levels: 4th–8th grades

Equipment: 1 tumbling mat

How to Play: For best results, instructors should pair the players by height. Partners sit directly across from each other with their feet approximately even with the hips of their partner.

One partner holds the heels of the other partner and lifts the legs above his or her head as if performing a shoulder press exercise. The partner being lifted keeps the legs straight and stays supported with the hands on the floor. When finished, have the partners switch roles.

Have each partner aim for a set number of presses.

Wheelbarrow Lifting

Introduction: Here is a nontraditional and fun way of accomplishing the squat exercise with a partner. Squats are one of the very best strength-building exercises for the legs.

Number of Players: 2

Suggested Grade Levels: K–8th grades

Equipment: 1 tumbling mat

How to Play: For best results, instructors should pair the players by size. The wheelbarrow partner assumes the wheelbarrow position, and the lifting partner grabs both of his/her legs.

The lifter holds the legs of the wheelbarrow partner and lifts the legs to the sides of the hips or waist area. The lifter then bends at the knees and goes down until the thighs are horizontal to the floor. At that point, the lifter comes up from the squatting position. The wheelbarrow partner being lifted keeps the legs straight and stays supported with the hands on the floor. Have the lifter aim for a set number of squats or lifts. When finished, have the partners switch roles.

Table Balance

Introduction: This is a natural progression from the Horizontal Balance (see page 150). It improves upper body strength and body control.

Number of Players: 2

Suggested Grade Levels: 3rd–8th grades

Equipment: 1 tumbling mat

How to Play: For best results, the instructor should pair players by size. The bottom support partner lies on the back with the legs apart and knees up. The hands are positioned close to the shoulders with the palms facing upward.

The top partner stands on the support partner's palms, leans forward, and places the hands on the support partner's knees. The support partner raises the top partner by lifting with the arms. The top partner is then in a "table" or all-fours position, with the hands supported by the support partner's knees and the feet supported by the support partner's extended arms and hands. The top partner should hold this pose for a few seconds. When finished, have the partners switch roles.

Over & Under Push-Ups

Introduction: This push-up variety will challenge your players and develop their upper body strength.

Number of Players: 2

Suggested Grade Levels: 1st–8th grades

Equipment: 1 tumbling mat

How to Play: One partner starts in a push-up position, and the other partner stands to the side ready to start crawling.

To begin, the push-up partner maintains a full push-up position while his/her partner crawls as quickly as possible underneath. The push-up partner then does a push-up and stands up. The crawling partner now gets into a push-up position and roles are reversed. With each push-up, the players call out the letters of the alphabet. The objective is to get to the letter "Z" as quickly as possible. An alternative way of keeping score of push-ups would be to simply do many as possible in a set amount of time (each push-up counting as one point).

Teeter-Totter Push-Ups

Introduction: Teeter-Totter Push-Ups calls for teamwork and effective communication as players perform push-ups in a nonconventional format. This is great activity for building upper body strength.

Number of Players: 2

Suggested Grade Levels: K–6th grades

Equipment: 1 tumbling mat

How to Play: One partner goes down on the mat into a regular push-up position. The other partner goes to the side of the push-up partner and places both feet on the flat portion of the partner's back. Both are now in a push-up position, but one partner has his feet supported and the other does not.

To begin, one partner performs a full push-up while the other partner watches. When finished, the partner that was watching now performs his or her push-up while the other player watches. The partners take turns going up and down performing their push-ups like a "teeter-totter." Have the pair aim for a predetermined number of joint push-ups.

Push-Up Twins

Introduction: Here's a fun challenge that will test your player's upper body strength!

Number of Players: 2

Suggested Grade Levels: 5th–8th grades

Equipment: 1 tumbling mat

How to Play: Match up pairs according to size and skill level. One partner goes down on the mat into a regular push-up position. The other partner goes to the side of the push-up partner and places his/her inside arm around the upper back of the partner's back. The first push-up player now does the same, placing his/her inside arm around that partner's upper back area. Both are now facing forward in a push-up position, and each has only hand on the floor

At the same time, both players go down and up performing push-ups. Since this is a very challenging activity, have the pair aim for a low number of joint push-ups in the beginning. With practice, they can try for higher and higher numbers.

Push-Up Centipede

Introduction: A strength-building activity that is both challenging and fun.

Number of Players: 2

Suggested Grade Levels: 2nd–8th grades

Equipment: 1 tumbling mat

How to Play: One partner goes down on the mat into the "flat" part of the push-up position. The other partner goes behind the push-up partner, places both his/her feet on the upper portion of the back, and lays flat on the mat. Both are now facing forward in a down or flat push-up position, but one partner has his feet supported and the other does not.

To begin, have both players go to the "up" position of a push-up. At this point, the back player can adjust the partner's feet so that they are securely resting on his/her back shoulder area. When ready, the partners perform as many push-ups as possible without falling.

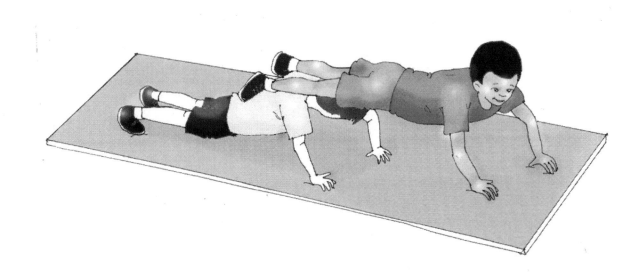

Push-Up High Fives

Introduction: Here's a partner alternative to performing push-ups or straight-arm planks that players will find both challenging and fun.

Number of Players: 2

Suggested Grade Levels: 1st–8th grades

Equipment: 1 tumbling mat

How to Play: Both partners go down on the mat facing each other in the push-up position about 3-5 feet apart.

To begin, both players try to alternately touch opposite hands (right to right, left to left) with a "high five" while maintaining a push-up position. With each hand slap or high five, the pair calls out the letters of the alphabet. The objective is to get to the letter "Z" as quickly as possible. An alternative way of keeping score of hand touches would be to simply do many as possible in a set amount of time (each touch counting as one point).

Crab High Fives

Introduction: Human crabs give "high fives" with their feet as they develop core strength.

Number of Players: 2

Suggested Grade Levels: 1st–8th grades

Equipment: 1 tumbling mat

How to Play: Both partners go down on the mat facing each other in a crab position about 2 feet apart.

To begin, both players try to alternately touch opposite feet (right to left, left to right) with the bottom of their feet while maintaining a crab position. With each touching of the bottom of the feet, the pair calls out the letters of the alphabet. The objective is to get to the letter "Z" as quickly as possible. An alternative way of keeping score of foot touches would be to simply do many as possible in a set amount of time (each touch counting as one point).

Beanbag Push-Ups

Introduction: This partner push-up game improves upper body strength, endurance, and eye-hand coordination.

Number of Players: 2

Suggested Grade Levels: 1st–6th grades

Equipment: 1 tumbling mat

How to Play: Both partners go down on the mat facing each other in the push-up position about 3-5 feet apart. One player begins with a beanbag.

To begin, the partner with the beanbag underhand tosses the beanbag from a push-up position to the other partner who tries to catch it while maintaining a push-up position. With each toss and catch, the pair calls out the letters of the alphabet. The objective is to get to the letter "Z" as quickly as possible. An alternative way of keeping score of tosses and catches would be to simply do many as possible in a set amount of time.

Push-Up Touchdowns

Introduction: Here's a terrific push-up variety to challenge your players. It develops upper body strength, improves eye-hand catching skills, and has a cardiovascular health benefit.

Number of Players: 2

Suggested Grade Levels: 4th–8th grades

Equipment: 1 tumbling mat, 1 beanbag

How to Play: One partner starts in a push-up position with a beanbag in one hand. The other partner stands directly their partner facing their partner's feet.

To begin, the partner without the beanbag (the "quarterback") yells out "ready, set, hike." The partner in the push-up position tosses the beanbag with one hand up and over their shoulder so that the quarterback can catch it (scoring a "touchdown"). After catching the beanbag, the quarterback runs forward and switches place with his/her partner. The previous push-up partner now becomes the new quarterback. Both players want to move as quickly as possible. With each tossed beanbag from the push-up partner, the pair keeps track of their score of tosses and catches. The objective is to score as many "touchdowns" as possible in a set time period.

Wheelbarrow Mat Tag

Introduction: Here is a unique tag game that uses a folded tumbling mat for developing shoulder, chest, and arm strength.

Number of Players: 2

Suggested Grade Levels: K–8th grades

Equipment: 1 tumbling mat

How to Play: This tag game for pairs requires an unfolded tumbling mat. Each player begins in a push-up position with the feet placed on top of the mat and the hands on the floor. Instead of the legs being held by a partner as in a real wheelbarrow, this game allows the mat to serve as the leg holder for each player. The players begin at opposite ends of the mat. Designate one player to start as the chaser or "It."

The activity begins with the "It" chasing the other player, trying to tag him or her on the hand. Both players have to walk on their hands the entire time. Since this is very tiring game, have the players take occasional breaks. Also, have the partners switch roles if a tag hasn't taken place after a set period of time.

Floor Routine Twins

Introduction: Here is a chance for your players to practice gymnastic floor routines with a partner. It's also a chance to let their imaginations and creativity take over!

Number of Players: 2

Suggested Grade Levels: K–8th grades

Equipment: 1 tumbling mat

How to Play: For the best results, pair the players by skill level and ability to communicate. To start, explain the floor routine event in gymnastics and what kinds of movements are involved. Additionally, showing pictures of each skill, or having an experienced player demonstrate the less complex skills that would be appropriate for younger players would be ideal. The objective for this activity is to mirror some of those movements with a partner.

Provide time for the partners to work cooperatively on a routine. Remind the players to choose movements for mirroring that are within their own and their partner's abilities. When the partners have selected a routine, check and make sure the skills are safe and appropriate for the age level of the players. Some of the mirror movement possibilities include running, leaping, galloping, skipping, and other simple locomotor movements. They can also perform various jumps together like the straddle jump, split jump, frog jump, pike jump, half turns, full turns, and so forth. Now, turn some music on and enjoy the floor routines!

Sport Duels

Finger Wrestling

Introduction: This is a fun and simple contest of balance in which two players use only their index fingers to "wrestle."

Number of Players: 2

Suggested Grade Levels: 3rd–8th grades

Equipment: None

How to Play: The partners start by facing each other standing on their right feet only. Next, they hook the index fingers on their right hands together.

On a signal, each player tries to pull and pull the opponent off balance using only the hooked index fingers. Any movement of the left supporting foot signifies a loss of point. After each turn, the players change the foot and hand positions and repeat play.

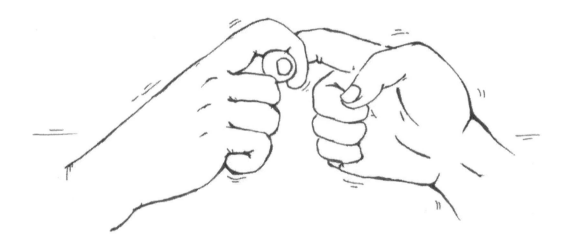

Skeet Feet

Introduction: Using a partner's foot for a skeet target, the players attempt to slide a beanbag and hit their target in an active and fun setting. This is a great energizer!

Number of Players: 2

Suggested Grade Levels: 1st–8th grades

Equipment: 2 beanbags

How to Play: Each player starts by facing their partner with a beanbag in hand.

On a signal, the players try to "tag" their partner by throwing the beanbag in an underhanded fashion at their feet while, at the same time, avoid being tagged. A player gets one point each time his or her beanbag hits one of the partner's feet. After each toss, players need to retrieve their beanbag and continue play. Players are only allowed to aim for the feet during play.

Seat Wrestling

Introduction: Here is a fun strength-building activity to use when players are starting to overheat but still need to be actively engaged.

Number of Players: 2

Suggested Grade Levels: 3rd–8th grades

Equipment: None

How to Play: The two players begin by facing each in a sitting position with their feet flat on the floor and toes touching. Next, they grasp both hands.

On a signal, the two players pull with their grasped hands (while sitting) and attempt to pull the opponent's bottom off the floor a few inches. If successful, a player is awarded one point. After each turn, the players resume their starting position and play again. Reinforce the need for players to stay seated on their bottom with both feet on the floor at all times. If the hands come apart while pulling, then no points are given and players start again.

Toe Fencing

Introduction: With its circling, feinting, and quick movements, here's a fun energizer that is reminiscent of the one-on-one sport of Fencing.

Number of Players: 2

Suggested Grade Levels: 3rd–8th grades

Equipment: None

How to Play: The players start by facing each other with the hands placed on the shoulders on the other player.

Using only feet, the players attempt to tag either foot of the opponent while, at the same time, keep their own feet from being tagged. Players can use a variety of circling and feinting movements before going for a quick touch with a foot, but must keep their hands on the opponent's shoulders throughout the contest. No kicking or stomping is allowed! Each successful tag counts as one point.

Knee Fencing

Introduction: Here is an imaginative form of Fencing in which partners try to score points by tagging each other's knees.

Number of Players: 2

Suggested Grade Levels: 3rd–8th grades

Equipment: None

How to Play: The players start by facing each other in a crouched position with right hands joined.

Using their free hand, the players attempt to tag either knee of the opponent while, at the same time, trying keep their own knees from being tagged. Players can use a variety of circling and feinting movements before going for a quick tag to the knee, but they must keep their right hands joined throughout the contest. Touching the knee with the open hand is the only kind of touch allowed. Each successful tag counts as one point. Have the players alternate their grasped hands after each contest.

Noodle Fencing

Introduction: Using noodles for Fencing, the players attempt to make a beanbag fall off the back of their partner's hand in a wild and fun setting. This is a great energizer!

Number of Players: 2

Suggested Grade Levels: 4th–8th grades

Equipment: 2 pool noodles, 2 beanbags

How to Play: The partners start by facing each other with a pool noodle in one hand and a beanbag balanced on the back of the other hand. The players keep the arm with the beanbag extended out to the side of their body.

On a signal, the players begin moving around the play area using their pool noodles to knock the beanbag off of the opponent's back hand. A player gets one point each time the opponent's beanbag drops to the floor. Once a player's beanbag falls, he or she picks it up and continues playing.

Players are only allowed to aim for the arm with the beanbag during play. No slapping with the noodle is allowed.

Hula Hoop Fencing

Introduction: Here is yet another fun and imaginative form of Fencing. In this version, players try to score points by knocking away a partner's hula hoop with their own.

Number of Players: 2

Suggested Grade Levels: 3rd–8th grades

Equipment: None

How to Play: Each partner begins by standing inside a hula hoop and facing each other a few feet apart.

Both players begin the game by hula hooping around their waist and advancing toward each other. While continuing to hoop, players use their own hoop to knock away their partner's hoop. The players can only make contact with the hoops. Each successful knock away of a hoop counts as a point. Play for a designated time period.

Hand Fencing

Introduction: Hand Fencing is a fun and vigorous activity for building upper-body strength.

Number of Players: 2

Suggested Grade Levels: 3rd–8th grades

Equipment: None

How to Play: The two players assume a push-up position facing each other about a foot apart.

On a signal, the players attempt to tag either hand of the opponent while, at the same time, keep their own hands from being tagged. Players can use a variety of circling and feinting movements before going for a quick touch, but must remain in a push-up position throughout the contest. Each successful tag counts as one point.

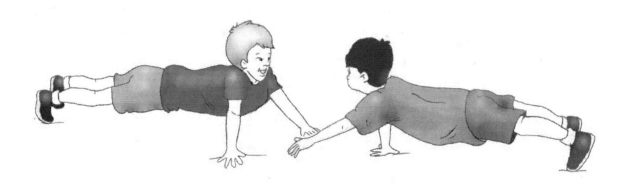

Bear Wrestling

Introduction: Bear Wrestling is a lively contest of quickness and endurance.

Number of Players: 2

Suggested Grade Levels: 4th–8th grades

Equipment: 1 flag set for each player, tape or chalk for marking

How to Play: With the chalk or tape, mark off a circle that is about 10-12 feet in diameter. The partners start in the middle facing each other in a "bear" position (on all fours), with a flag hanging from the back of their belt or pants.

The objective is to win the contest by pulling the opponent's flag. The contest begins with the players circling and making a variety of quick movements to position themselves for a pull of the opponent's flag. Players are to stay on all fours in a bear position (that is, they are not allowed to stand up), and have to stay inside the circle at all times. No grabbing, kicking, or any form of rough play is allowed.

Crab Wrestling

Introduction: Crab Wrestling improves muscular strength in the legs, arms, shoulders, and back.

Number of Players: 2

Suggested Grade Levels: 3rd–8th grades

Equipment: None

How to Play: The two players begin in a crab position with the hands and feet on the floor and the front of the bodies facing upward.

On a signal, the two human crabs use their feet and hands in grabbing and pulling movements to force the opponent's bottom to touch the floor. If successful, a player is awarded one point. After each turn, the players return to crab position and resume play.

For safety purposes, reinforce that only grabbing and pulling movements can be used. Players are not allowed to kick, punch, or exhibit any type of unsafe behavior.

Flamingo Wrestling

Introduction: This contest of human flamingos tests players' strength and balance.

Number of Players: 2

Suggested Grade Levels: 4th–8th grades

Equipment: 1 tumbling mat

How to Play: Place a mat on the floor. The partners start in the middle of the mat facing each other in a one-legged standing position (that is, each stands on their right foot with the left foot off the ground and being held with the left hand).

The objective is to win the contest by pulling and making the opponent let go of his or her left foot or touch the ground with any part of the body other than the right foot. To begin, have the players face each other, each holding his or her left foot off the ground. The players grasp right hands, and on a signal, try to pull and force each other off balance. Players are allowed to hop about, but cannot let go of their joined right hands or let go of their own left foot. Players have to stay on the mat at all times and no grabbing, kicking, or any form of rough play is allowed.

Rope Jousting

Introduction: Rope Jousting is a modification of an Early American game called Rooks. Using a rope for the jousting, the players push and pull with strength and balance.

Number of Players: 2

Suggested Grade Levels: 4th–8th grades

Equipment: 1 rope (about 10 feet in length), 2 hula hops

How to Play: Place two hula hoops about six feet apart with a player positioned inside each one. The players are given a rope (about 10 feet in length), with each holding the rope so that an extra part of the rope (1-2 feet) is hanging from their hands.

The objective is to unbalance the opponent so that he or she steps out of the hoop. On a starting signal, the two players begin pulling, as well as letting the rope slip a little, so that the other player loses balance and steps with at least one foot outside of the hoop.

Unlike tug-o-war, strength is not the only factor to winning in jousting. Keeping one's balance during the opponent's rope slips is an important factor. However, when executing a rope slip, at no time can a player completely let go of the rope so that it falls to the ground.

Noodle Jousting

Introduction: Using a noodle for the jousting, the players push and pull with strength and balance.

Number of Players: 2

Suggested Grade Levels: 4th–8th grades

Equipment: 1 pool noodle

How to Play: The partners start by facing each other, with their right feet touching and their left feet planted firmly behind on the ground for support. They both grasp one end of the noodle.

On a signal, the players begin pulling and pushing the noodle to get the other player to lose his or her balance. The players can shake, feint, and yank the noodle, but are not allowed to drop the noodle or make contact with the other player with the hands. Players have to keep their inside feet together at all times. The first player who lifts either foot off the ground loses the match.

Crab Jousting

Introduction: Using a leg for the jousting, the human crabs push and feint with endurance, strength, and balance.

Number of Players: 2

Suggested Grade Levels: 4th–8th grades

Equipment: None

How to Play: The two players begin in a crab position. They then position the bottom of their right feet together in the air (after which they will be balancing their crab position from the two hands and left foot). Remind the players to keep their bottoms high off the floor.

The objective is to unbalance the opponent so that his or her bottom comes in contact with the floor. On a starting signal, the two players begin pushing with their right feet against each other, as well as easing up with the foot pressure, so that the other player loses balance. Players change the jousting foot after each round.

Unlike tug-o-war, strength is not the only factor to winning in jousting. Keeping one's balance during the opponent's easing of foot pressure is an important factor.

Push-Up Hockey

Introduction: This is one my students' favorites for building body strength and endurance.

Number of Players: 2

Suggested Grade Levels: 3rd–8th grades

Equipment: 1 beanbag

How to Play: Form a group of two players. The two "hockey" players should be facing each other about five feet apart in a push-up position (arms fully extended). Designate one player to start with the beanbag (the "puck").

On a signal, the player with the beanbag attempts to slide it through the arms (the "hockey goal") of the opponent for a score. The opponent can block the beanbag with a hand, but must remain in a push-up position while doing so. Player alternate turns at scoring with each attempt. Each successful slide of the beanbag through the opponent's arms counts as one point.

Wheelbarrow Hockey

Introduction: This challenging game uses the strategy of hockey and is played with human wheelbarrows. It's not only fun, it's a great activity for building body strength and endurance.

Number of Players: 4

Suggested Grade Levels: 4th–8th grades

Equipment: 1 beanbag

How to Play: Form two teams of two players each. The partner on each team acting as the wheelbarrow goes down on his or her hands in a push-up position. The other partners pick up the legs of the wheelbarrows. The two wheelbarrows should be facing each other about a foot apart. Designate one wheelbarrow team to start with the beanbag (the "puck").

On a signal, the wheelbarrow player with the beanbag attempts to slide it through the arms (the "hockey goal") of the opposing wheelbarrow for a score. The opponent can block the beanbag with a hand, but must remain in a wheelbarrow position while doing so. Each successful slide of the beanbag through the opponent's arms counts as one point.

Because this game can be very tiring, have the partners switch positions often.

Push-Up Soccer

Introduction: This is a one-on-one soccer game played in a push-up position with a foam ball. Push-up Soccer is a tremendous builder of upper body strength, endurance, body control, and eye-hand coordination.

Number of Players: 2

Suggested Grade Levels: 3rd–8th grades

Equipment: 1 foam ball, 4 cones

How to Play: For the goals, place two cones (about 5 feet apart) at each end of the play area which is about 8 feet in length. Assign two players to the play area. The two "soccer goalie" players should be facing each other from the front of their goals in a push-up position (arms fully extended). Designate one player to start with the ball.

On a signal, the player with the ball maintains a push-up position and attempts to roll it through the goal (the cones) of the opponent for a score. The opponent can block the ball with a hand, but must remain in a push-up position while doing so. Both players must stay in front of their goals and are not allowed to advance toward the other player. Player alternate turns at scoring with each attempt. Each successful roll of the ball through the opponent's goal counts as one point.

Crab Soccer Duel

Introduction: This one-on-one game is played in a crab position with a foam ball. Like its counterpart, Push-up Soccer, it's a tremendous builder of upper body strength, endurance, body control, and eye-foot coordination.

Number of Players: 2

Suggested Grade Levels: 3rd–8th grades

Equipment: 1 foam ball, 4 cones

How to Play: For the goals, place two cones (about 5 feet apart) at each end of the play area which is about 8 feet in length. Assign two players the play area. The two "soccer goalie" players should be facing each other from the front of their goals in a crab position (hands and feet on the ground with the upper torso facing upward). Designate one player to start with the ball.

On a signal, the player with the ball maintains a crab position and attempts to kick it through the goal (the two cones) of the opponent for a score,. The opponent can block the ball with a hand or foot, but must remain in a crab position while doing so. Both players stay in front of their goals and are not allowed to cross the midfield of the play area. Player alternate turns at scoring with each attempt. Each successful kick of the ball through the opponent's cones counts as one point.

Speed Bag Duel

Introduction: Speed Bag Duel is a "camouflaged" fitness game that develops upper body strength, quickness, and laterality skills. Because it's so much fun, players won't even know this a plank exercise unless you tell them!

Number of Players: 2

Suggested Grade Levels: 3rd–8th grades

Equipment: 1 beanbag

How to Play: The two players assume a push-up position facing each other about a foot apart. A beanbag is placed on the floor in the middle of the players.

The instructor begins by calling out "ready," which informs the players to be in the up position of a push-up. At any time, the instructor can call out "right," or "left." The players, while in a push-up position, react quickly by reaching for the beanbag with the hand that was called. One point is given to the player who first grabs the beanbag. Repeat several times.

Variation: To provide a "rest break" during the Speed Bag Duel, consider playing a sitting version. Instead of a push-up position, both players sit with their legs crossed and facing each other. The beanbag is grabbed in the same fashion as in Speed Bag Duel.

Wheelbarrow Fencing

Introduction: Making a wheelbarrow with a partner has always been a favorite with my students. The "fencing" with the hands adds additional excitement, challenge, and fun.

Number of Players: 4

Suggested Grade Levels: 4th–8th grades

Equipment: None

How to Play: Form two teams of two players each. The partner on each team acting as the wheelbarrow goes down on his or her hands in a push-up position. The other partners pick up the legs of the wheelbarrows. The two wheelbarrows should be facing each other about a foot apart.

On a signal, the wheelbarrow players attempt to tag either hand of the opponent while, at the same time, keep their own hands from being tagged. Wheelbarrow teams can use a variety of circling and feinting movements before going for a quick touch, but must remain in a wheelbarrow position throughout the contest. Each successful tag counts as one point. After a short period of time, have the partners switch positions and resume play.

Sports
of
Sorts!

Kickball Duel

Introduction: This one-on-one game eliminates the sedentary nature of playing regular Kickball.

Number of Players: 2

Suggested Grade Levels: K–4th grades

Equipment: 1 playground ball, 2 bases

How to Play: The play area consists of two bases placed approximately 20-30 feet apart. Designate one base as the "home" base and the other as the "far" base. There are no boundary lines. One player begins as the kicker while the other player starts as the pitcher.

The game begins with the pitcher gently rolling the ball toward the kicker. After kicking the ball, the kicker attempts to run to the far base and back before the pitcher retrieves the ball and touches home base. One point (or "run") is awarded to the kicker if he or she beats the pitcher to home base. Likewise, no point is given if the pitcher arrives at home base before the kicker. There are no outs for tagging a runner or catching a fly ball. The players reverse roles after each play.

Kickball Doubles

Introduction: This two-on-two activity maximizes ball handling and kicking opportunities. It's a natural progression from Kickball Duel (one-on-one kickball).

Number of Players: 4

Suggested Grade Levels: K–4th grades

Equipment: 1 playground ball, 2 bases

How to Play: The play area consists of two bases placed approximately 30-40 feet apart. Designate one base as the "home" base and the other as the "far" base. There are no boundary lines. Form two teams of two players each. One team begins as kickers while the other team starts as the fielders.

The game begins with the pitcher rolling the playground ball gently toward home base. The kicker's objective is to make it safely to the far base, where he/she can choose to stop and wait for the next kicker to hit him/her home, or to the far base and back without stopping. A run is awarded each time a player runs to the far base and back to home base. A kicker is put out if a fielder catches a fly ball or if tagged with the ball while running the bases. A kicker can also be put out if the fielding team tags the far base before he or she arrives (which introduces the concept of the "force" out). There is no base stealing and base runners are not allowed to lead off. The teams switch places after three outs.

Kickball Triplets

Introduction: This three-player game develops throwing, catching, and kicking skills. It also allows players to practice the concept of working together to get a kicker out.

Number of Players: 3

Suggested Grade Levels: K–4th grades

Equipment: 1 playground ball, 2 bases

How to Play: The play area consists of two bases placed approximately 30-40 feet apart. Designate one base as the "home" base and the other as the "far" base. There are no boundary lines. Designate one player to begin as the kicker, one player as the pitcher, and one player as the outfielder.

The game begins with the pitcher gently rolling the playground ball toward home base. The kicker kicks the ball out into the field in any direction (there are no boundary lines) and begins running around the two bases. The kicker counts the number of times he or she circles the far base and home base. The kicker's objective is to make it safely to the far base and back to home as many times possible without stopping. A run is awarded each time a player runs to the far base and back to home base.

A kicker is put out if a fielder catches a fly ball or if tagged with the ball while running the bases. A kicker can also be put out if the fielding team tags the far base or home base before the kicker arrives (which introduces the concept of two fielders working together to get a "force" out). After each play, the players rotate positions. The kicker moves to outfield, the outfielder to infielder, and the infielder becomes the next kicker.

Mini Kickball

Introduction: This three-on-three game, with its smaller play area and fewer players, maximizes ball handling, running, and kicking opportunities versus playing regular Kickball.

Number of Players: 6

Suggested Grade Levels: K–6th grades

Equipment: 1 playground ball, 3 bases

How to Play: The triangular-shaped play area consists of three bases placed approximately 30-40 feet apart. Designate one base as the "home" base and the other as first and second bases. There are no boundary lines. Form two teams of three players each. One team begins as kickers while the other team starts as the fielders (a pitcher, infielder, and outfielder).

The game begins with the pitcher rolling the playground ball gently toward home base. The kicker's objective is to make it safely to first or second base, where he/she can choose to stop and wait for the next kicker to hit him/her home, or around both bases without stopping. A run is awarded each time a player runs around both bases and back to home base. A kicker is put out if a fielder catches a fly ball or if tagged with the ball while running the bases. A kicker can also be put out if the fielding team tags the base before he or she arrives on a "force" out situation. There is no base stealing and base runners are not allowed to lead off. The teams switch places after three outs.

Aerobic Bowling

Introduction: Aerobic Bowling develops the rolling accuracy needed in bowling while providing plenty of continuous movement.

Number of Players: 2

Suggested Grade Levels: K–6th grades

Equipment: 1 foam bowling ball (or substitute a small playground ball), 1 bowling pin

How to Play: Set up a "bowling lane" with a bowling pin approximately 30 feet from the spot where the bowler stands. This distance can vary depending on the age and skill level of the players. One player stands behind the pin ready to set it back up, and the other player stands ready to bowl.

Aerobic Bowling is essentially the game of bowling with one pin instead of ten, and each bowler is allowed to bowl once (not twice at a time). The first bowler attempts to roll the ball and knock over the stationary bowling pin to score a strike (one point). After releasing the ball, the bowler runs toward the pin and switches place with his or her teammate. The pin set-up player retrieves the ball and immediately runs toward the bowling line to roll the ball. Players switch positions after each roll. The objective is to have the highest number of strikes after predetermined time period.

Frisbee Bowling

Introduction: Frisbee Bowling develops throwing accuracy while providing lots of movement. Players also have the opportunity to use the terminology and scoring of regular bowling.

Number of Players: 2

Suggested Grade Levels: K–6th grades

Equipment: 2 frisbees, 10 bowling pins

How to Play: Set up a "bowling lane" with the 10 bowling pins approximately 30 feet from the spot where the thrower stands. This distance can vary depending on the age and skill level of the players. One player stands behind the pins ready to set back up any knocked over pins, and the other player stands ready to throw the frisbee.

Frisbee Bowling is essentially the game of bowling with a frisbee being used instead of a rolled ball. The first bowler attempts to throw and knock down as many pins as possible. The objective is to gain a strike by knocking all of the pins down, or to knock over as many as possible by the second throw. After the second throw, the bowler switches with the pin set-up player. Each bowler is allowed two throws per frame, with 10 frames in each game. Scoring is the same as in bowling.

Bowling Sliders

Introduction: Bowling Sliders is an ideal game for introducing young players to the strategy of bowling. The familiarity of the underhand tossing motion and the fact that beanbags are much easier to handle than a regular bowling ball assures a higher level success and enjoyment.

Number of Players: 2

Suggested Grade Levels: K–4th grades

Equipment: 2 beanbags, 3 bowling pins

How to Play: Set up a "bowling lane" with the 3 bowling pins approximately 30 feet from the spot where the thrower (the bowler) stands. This distance can vary depending on the age and skill level of the players. One player stands behind the pins ready to set back up any knocked over pins, and the other player stands ready to underhand toss a beanbag.

Bowling Sliders is essentially the game of bowling with a beanbag being used instead of a rolled ball. The first bowler attempts to underhand throw the beanbag in a fashion that it slides on the floor and knocks down as many pins as possible. The objective is to gain a strike by knocking all of the pins down, or to knock over as many as possible by the second throw. A bowler gets one point for each pin knocked over. After the second throw, the bowler switches with the pin set-up player. Each bowler is allowed two throws per frame, with 10 frames in each game.

Beanbag Bocce

Introduction: Beanbag Bocce is a modified version of Bocce, a popular game that originated in Italy. It is also considered the front-runner to the sport of Bowling.

Number of Players: 2

Suggested Grade Levels: K–4th grades

Equipment: 4 beanbags, 1 plastic whiffle ball

How to Play: Set aside a play area that is approximately 10 feet by 30 feet in size. Designate one end as the throwing line. Place the plastic whiffle ball at the opposite end for the "center ball." Each game has one pair of players. Two beanbags of a different color are required by each player.

In turn, the players throw or slide their two beanbags at the whiffle ball (which serves as the center ball), with the objective of hitting it or landing the beanbags closest to it. Scores are calculated after all of the beanbags have been thrown. The player who has a beanbag hit the ball or lands closest to it receives three points. The next closest receives two points, and the third closest receives one point. It is possible for a single player to receive two scores because each player has two throw attempts. As in regular Bocce, it is legal and considered good strategy to knock an opponent's beanbag away from the ball. Play continues in this fashion until one player has reached fifteen points.

Beanbag Golf

Introduction: Beanbag Golf develops the skill of underhand throwing while using the strategies and scoring of playing regular golf.

Number of Players: 2

Suggested Grade Levels: 1st–6th grades

Equipment: 1 beanbag for each player, 9 hula hoops, 9 numbered cones

How to Play: Assign two players to a course (for a larger group, assign two players to start at each hole). Design a golf course by placing the hula hoops with a numbered cone inside (1 through 9) in a scattered formation around the gym or play area. Players establish a throwing order. If needed, give each player a scorecard and pencil.

The game begins with each player, in turn, underhand tossing a beanbag toward hole #1, trying to land it inside the hula hoop. The number of shots needed to make the "hole" is recorded for each player. When finished, the group moves to hole #2 and each player continues to throw and land the beanbag inside the hula hoop in as few attempts possible. The objective is to finish the course by having the lowest score (that is, the fewest throws).

Frisbee Golf

Introduction: Here's a fun version of golf that doesn't require green fees, clubs, or golf balls—just an ordinary frisbee, a few hula hoops, and some imagination! Besides frisbee throwing, players also learn golf strategy and etiquette.

Number of Players: 2

Suggested Grade Levels: 3rd–8h grades

Equipment: 1 frisbee for each player, 9 hula hoops, 9 numbered cones

How to Play: Assign two players to a course (for a larger group, assign two players to start at each hole). Design a golf course by placing the hula hoops with a numbered cone inside (1 through 9) in a scattered formation around the gym or play area. Players establish a throwing order. If needed, give each player a scorecard and pencil.

The game begins with each player, in turn, tossing a frisbee toward hole #1, trying to land it inside the hula hoop. The number of shots needed to make the "hole" is recorded for each player. When finished, the group moves to hole #2 and each player continues to throw and land the frisbee inside the hula hoop in as few attempts possible. The objective is to finish the course by having the lowest score (that is, the fewest throws).

Variation: Instead of using hula hoops for the holes, consider designing a "putt-putt" course using natural or playground objects such as trees, benches, shrubs, poles, playground equipment, and so forth.

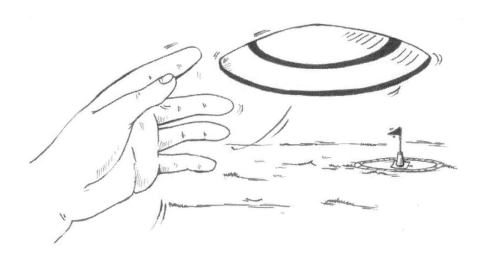

Foxtail Horseshoes

Introduction: This modified version of Horseshoes provides a simple, safe, and fun game setting. Foxtails and hula hoops replace the iron posts and heavy metal shoes that are normally used.

Number of Players: 2

Suggested Grade Levels: K–6th grades

Equipment: 2 Foxtails, 2 hula hoops

How to Play: Place two hula hoops approximately 20-30 feet apart (however, the distance can vary depending on the age of the players). Position one player behind each hoop and give each player two Foxtails (a tube sock with a ball at the end).

This game is played much like regular horseshoes with the same rules and strategy. When throwing, players must stay behind their hoop. The throws are done with an underhanded motion, with the objective of landing the Foxtail inside the hoop for a "ringer." Each player is allowed two throws. A ringer counts as three points. Two points is awarded if the Foxtail is touching the hoop. One point is awarded if a Foxtail ends up being the closest to a hoop without being a ringer. The first player to score fifteen points wins the game.

Hula Hoop Quoits

Introduction: Hoop Quoits is an adaptation of the regular game of Quoits. Instead of using wood stakes and a rubber donut-shaped ring, this version requires only small hula hoops and cones.

Number of Players: 2

Suggested Grade Levels: K–8th grades

Equipment: 4 small hula hoops, 2 cones

How to Play: Place two cones approximately 20-30 feet apart (however, the distance can vary depending on the age of the players). Position one player behind each cone and give each player two small hula hoops.

This game is played much like regular horseshoes with the same rules and strategy. When throwing, players must stay behind their hoop. The throws are done with a sideways motion, with the objective of landing the hoop on the cone for a "ringer." Each player is allowed two throws. A ringer counts as three points. Two points is awarded if the hoop is touching or leaning on the cone. One point is awarded if the hoop ends up being the closest to a cone without being a ringer. The first player to score fifteen points wins the game.

Wall Ball

Introduction: Wall Ball is a classic game that remains a favorite on the playground. Speed, agility, and hand-eye coordination are enhanced through the striking of the ball with the hands.

Number of Players: 2

Suggested Grade Levels: 1st–6th grades

Equipment: 1 playground ball, marking tape (or chalk for marking a court outside)

How to Play: The game requires a flat surface adjacent to a wall. Mark off two boundary lines extending straight out from the wall that are about 12-15 feet in width. A short line, about five feet from the wall, should also be marked (sideline to sideline). Assign two players to the play area, and hand one player the ball.

The player with the ball begins as the server. The server stands behind the short line and starts play by throwing the ball against the wall, letting it bounce once on the ground before making contact with the wall. The opponent tries to catch the ball in the air after it bounces off the wall. If successful, he or she becomes the next server. If not, the server receives one point and continues serving. A fault is called if a throw does not hit the ground before hitting the wall, or if a throw does not clear the short line. After two faults, the serve changes to the other player. The first player to fifteen points wins.

Water Skiing Partners

Introduction: This strength-building activity is a favorite of my students. One partner "water skis," while the other partner acts as the "boat."

Number of Players: 2

Suggested Grade Levels: 3rd–8th grades

Equipment: 1 carpet square, 1 rope (10 feet or longer)

How to Play: Group the players into pairs. Hand each pair of players a carpet square (free at most carpet stores) and one rope.

One partner gets into a "water skiing" position by standing with both feet on the inverted carpet square in a crouched position. The water skier also holds both ends of the rope tightly. The other partner is the "boat" and stands inside the other end of the rope (holding it around the waist). The two partners work together to travel around the gym. The boat must pull using his or her legs to move the water skier, and the water skier needs to stay as balanced as possible. After a time in the standing position, have the water skier try a different position such as sitting or kneeling. For the most success and fun, remind the players not to go too fast or to jerk the rope if acting as the boat. Have the partners switch roles after a certain time period.

Noodle Darts

Introduction: This is a safe and fun simulation of playing Darts on a larger scale. The use of pool noodles and a hula hoop substitute for the use of regular darts and a dartboard.

Number of Players: 2

Suggested Grade Levels: 2nd–8th grades

Equipment: 2 pool noodles, 1 hula hoop

How to Play: Using an open area, have two players stand at opposite ends of a play area that is about 12 feet apart. One partner holds a hula hoop high above his or her head in a stationary position. The other partner has two pool noodles and is facing the hula hoop from the opposite end.

The strategy is much like Darts. The thrower has two chances to throw the noodles through the hula hoop for a "bulls-eye". The partner has to stand stationary and cannot move the hula hoop (the "dartboard") during a throw. One point is awarded to the thrower for each noodle that travels through the hoop. After every two throws, the partners rotate positions.

Handball Tennis

Introduction: This unique game is a combination of Handball, Tennis, and Two-Square. Speed, agility, and hand-eye coordination are skills enhanced through the striking of the tennis ball.

Number of Players: 2

Suggested Grade Levels: 2nd–8th grades

Equipment: 1 tennis ball, marking tape (or chalk for marking a court outside)

How to Play: With the marking tape or chalk, make a court which is rectangular shaped (about 8 feet by 5 feet) and looks similar to a Two-Square court. A center line is drawn and divides the court into two equal halves. Have two players position themselves on opposite sides of the court. Have the players decide who will serve first.

This game follows the same basic rules of tennis, but without rackets and a net. The first server stands anywhere on his or her half of the court and serves the ball by bouncing it once and hitting it with an open palm. The ball must go over the center line and bounce once within the boundaries of the opponent's court before it is returned. The players slap the ball back and forth in the same open-palm manner until someone loses the volley by missing the ball, hitting it out of bounds, or not hitting it over the center line.

If the server loses the volley, the other player gets to serve, but does not receive a point. If the nonserver loses the volley, the server gets a point and continues to serve. As in tennis, a player can only score when he or she is serving. The goal is to be the first player to reach eleven points.

Speedball Hoops

Introduction: This enjoyable game is a modification of regular Speedball and develops both passing and catching skills.

Number of Players: 6

Suggested Grade Levels: 4rd–8th grades

Equipment: 1 medium-size foam ball, 2 hula hoops

How to Play: This game can be played on a regular basketball court, or any part of the court. Place a hula hoop on the floor at end of the play area for the goals. Form two teams of three players each. Designate one team to start on offense with the ball. Have each player choose an opposing player to guard.

Play begins with the offensive team advancing the ball down the court by throwing and catching, and attempts to score (one point) by throwing the ball so that hits inside the opponent's hula hoop. Offensive players with possession of the ball are able to run freely until tagged by a defensive player. At this point, the tagged player has to stop immediately and either pass or shoot the ball within five seconds. Defensive players cannot steal the ball out of the hands of an offensive player, but they can intercept or knock away a pass. Additionally, no defensive player is allowed to stand inside the hoop they are guarding. Each team must complete three passes before a shot attempt. Following each score, the non-scoring team takes immediate possession and begins play going in the opposite direction.

Indoor Polo

Introduction: This enjoyable game simulates the sport of Polo. In this modification, the pool noodle replicates the use of a regular polo stick.

Number of Players: 6

Suggested Grade Levels: 3rd–8th grades

Equipment: 1 pool noodle for each player, 1 whiffle ball, 4 cones

How to Play: Place two cones (for goals) at opposite ends of the play area. The whiffle ball is set in the middle of the play area. There are no boundary lines. Arrange the players into two equal teams of three players each. The players start with a noodle in hand on their side of the court.

On a signal, the players move toward the whiffle ball and attempt to advance the ball by toward their goal for a score. One point is scored when the ball passes through the opponent's two cones. Since there are no boundary lines, a score can be made from either side of the cones. Passes and shots can only be made with the noodle (that is, players cannot advance the ball or make a shot with their feet or hands). Play continues in this fashion for a predetermined number of points or time.

Push-Up Pinball

Introduction: Here is another "camouflaged" fitness game that uses the same muscles in the upper body as the push-up or plank exercise.

Number of Players: 6

Suggested Grade Levels: 3rd–8th grades

Equipment: 1 small foam ball

How to Play: Form two teams of three players each. The two teams form a circle with three players on one half and the other team on the other half circle. The players should be facing the middle of the circle in a push-up position (arms fully extended). The arms represent goals and together they pretend to be a pinball machine. Designate one player to start with the foam ball (the "pinball").

On a signal, the player with the ball slaps it and tries to roll it through the arms of one the opposing team members for a score. The opponents can block the ball with a hand, but must remain in a push-up position while doing so. Each successful roll of the ball through the opponent's arms counts as one point.

After a while, consider adding more foam balls!

Skeet Targets

Introduction: This imaginative game develops throwing accuracy.

Number of Players: 2

Suggested Grade Levels: 2nd–8th grades

Equipment: 2 foam balls, 1 hula hoop

How to Play: Using an open area, have two players stand at opposite ends of a play area that is about 12 feet apart. One partner holds a hula hoop (the "skeet") and is ready to toss it on command. The other partner has two foam balls and is facing the skeet from the opposite end.

The strategy is much like hitting a regular skeet target. The thrower has two chances to throw the balls through the moving hula hoop for a score (one point). After the thrower yells out "Go," the partner holding the hula hoop throws it straight up a few feet in the air. The thrower then attempts to throw the ball through the middle of the hoop while it is moving in the air. One point is awarded to the thrower for each ball that travels through the hoop. After every two throws, the partners rotate positions.

Skeet Throwing

Introduction: Skeet Throwing develops throwing accuracy and provides lots of excitement.

Number of Players: 2

Suggested Grade Levels: 3rd–8th grades

Equipment: 1 beach ball (or balloon), 1 foam frisbee

How to Play: Have the players work in pairs. One partner holds a beach ball (the "skeet") and is ready to toss it on command. The other partner has two foam frisbees (available in most physical education catalogs) and is facing the beach ball holder from a few feet away.

The strategy is much like the game of Skeet Targets (see previous page). The thrower has two chances to throw the frisbees at a moving beach ball for a score. After the thrower yells out "Go," the partner holding the beach ball throws it straight up a few feet in the air. The thrower then attempts to hit the beach ball with the frisbee while it is moving in the air. One point is awarded to the thrower for each Frisbee that hits a beach ball. After every two throws, the partners rotate positions.

Mini Ultimate

Introduction: This fitness-building game is played somewhat like the regular game of Frisbee Ultimate with the exception that far fewer players are required. Passing and catching are the principle skills developed.

Number of Players: 6

Suggested Grade Levels: 4rd–8th grades

Equipment: 1 frisbee, 4 cones

How to Play: With the cones, mark off a rectangular shaped play area. The two cones at the ends represent the goal lines. Organize two teams of three players each. Both teams start by facing each other on in the middle of the play area. Designate one team to start on defense and the other team to start on offense with the frisbee. Each player should choose an opposing player to guard throughout the game.

The team objective is to have a player catch a frisbee past the opponent's goal line for a score (one point). The player on offense with the frisbee starts the game by passing to teammate. Since players with possession of the frisbee cannot run with it, the frisbee is advanced down the field by a combination of completed passes. Upon catching a pass, a player has only two steps to come to a complete stop or else a violation is called. Additionally, passers have only five seconds to throw the Frisbee or a violation is also called. A violation results in the other team taking possession of the frisbee at that spot, and they now try to advance the frisbee offensively toward the opposite goal line. As long as the offensive team successfully catches the frisbee, they have an unlimited number of plays to score. Besides the violations mentioned above, any thrown or dropped frisbee that touches the ground also results in the other team taking possession.

Lacrosse Doubles

Introduction: This is a safe version of lacrosse that can be played by young players and those with little lacrosse experience. The use of plastic scoops and a whiffle ball develops many of the throwing and catching skills used in lacrosse.

Number of Players: 4

Suggested Grade Levels: 4th–8th grades

Equipment: 1 scoop for each player, 1 whiffle ball, 2 cones

How to Play: Place two cones about 30-50 feet apart (this distance can vary depending on the age of the players). There are no boundary lines. Form two teams of two players each. Each player has a plastic scoop. Designate one team to start with the ball (in one of the players' scoops) near the cone they are defending.

The game begins with the offensive players moving and passing the ball with their scoops toward the opponent's goal (the cone). The objective is to hit the opponent's cone with the ball either in the air or on the ground for a score (one point). Players can move anywhere with the ball since there are no boundary lines. The defensive players are allowed to guard the offensive players and can knock down or intercept any pass attempt. However, defensive players are not allowed to make any physical contact. After each score, the non-scoring team begins play again with the ball near their cone.

Lacrosse Ultimate

Introduction: This lead-up game is played somewhat like the regular game of Frisbee Ultimate, with the exception that plastic scoops and a whiffle ball are used instead of a frisbee.

Number of Players: 6

Suggested Grade Levels: 4rd–8th grades

Equipment: 1 plastic scoop for each player, 1 whiffle ball, cones

How to Play: With the cones, mark off a rectangular shaped play area. The two cones at the ends represent the goal lines. Organize two teams of three players each. Both teams start by facing each other on in the middle of the play area, and all players have a plastic scoop in hand to replicate a lacrosse stick. Designate one team to start on defense and the other team to start on offense with the ball. Each player should choose an opposing player to guard throughout the game.

The team objective is to have a player catch the whiffle ball with his or her scoop past the opponent's goal line for a score (one point). The player on offense with the ball starts the game by passing to teammate. The ball is both caught and thrown with the scoop. Since players with possession of the ball cannot run with it, the ball is advanced down the field by a combination of completed passes. Upon catching a pass, a player has only two steps to come to a complete stop or else a violation is called. Additionally, passers have only five seconds to throw the ball or a violation is also called. A violation results in the other team taking possession of the ball at that spot, and they now try to advance the ball offensively toward the opposite goal line. As long as the offensive team successfully catches the ball with a scoop, they have an unlimited number of plays to score. Besides the violations mentioned above, any thrown or dropped ball that touches the ground also results in the other team taking possession.

Lacrosse Golf

Introduction: This golf-type game requires players to advance through the golf holes by passing and catching a whiffle ball back and forth with plastic scoops.

Number of Players: 2

Suggested Grade Levels: 4th–8th grades

Equipment: 2 scoops and 1 whiffle ball for each pair, nine bowling pins (or substitute cones)

How to Play: Assign two players to a course (for a larger group, assign two players to start at each hole). Design a golf course by placing a numbered cone (1 through 9) in a scattered formation around the play area. Players start with a plastic scoop in hand and establish a striking order.

The object of Lacrosse Golf is for the two teammates to move to each cone (or golf hole) by completing a series of passes and catches. The player (#1) without the whiffle ball begins play by running any distance toward the first hole, and then stops to receive a pass from his teammate (using the scoop). After making a catch or retrieving the ball, player #1 stands stationary at that spot. Meanwhile, player #2 after initially throwing the ball runs closer to the cone and receives a pass from play #1. Play continues in this fashion until the pair has completed a hole by hitting the cone with the whiffle ball. Missed shots at the cone count as a "stroke," and the total of all the missed shots (not the passes and catches) equals the score for that hole. Having as few strokes as possible for the entire course is the goal for each pair.

Mini Danish Rounders

Introduction: This fun outdoor game is a simplified and compact version of regular Danish Rounders. The game calls for good throwing and catching skills, and the ability to strike a tennis ball with a hand.

Number of Players: 6

Suggested Grade Levels: 3rd–8th grades

Equipment: 1 tennis ball, chalk or tape for marking lines and bases

How to Play: The play area looks very much like a small softball infield. With the chalk or tape, draw up lines and boxes to represent first base, second base, third base, home base, and foul lines. The sides are about 15 feet in length. The players divide into two equal teams of three players each. The team in the "field" begins in the positions of pitcher, catcher, and outfielder. The three members of the batting team stand off the infield in a batting order.

Play begins with the pitcher throwing the tennis ball underhanded to the first batter. With a hand, the batter attempts to hit the tennis ball out into the field. The batter is allowed only one swat. A miss or poor hit still results in the batter running toward first base. The base runner can keep running until the pitcher has the ball, puts it on the ground, and yells out "Down." If the base runner is not on a base, he or she is out. If standing on a base at the time of the yell, then the base runner is safe. Once the base runner has stopped at a base and the ball has been downed, he or she waits there until the next player hits, at which point he or she can run to the next base. Runs are scored when players make it safely around all three bases and touch home base. The teams switch sides after three outs.

Mini Team Handball

Introduction: This is a very active game that has been modified from the regular version of Handball. Players will enjoy the challenging nature of this throwing and catching activity.

Number of Players: 6

Suggested Grade Levels: 4rd–8th grades

Equipment: 1 medium-size foam ball, 2 tumbling mats

How to Play: This game can be played on a regular basketball court, or any part of the court. Place a tumbling mat upright at end of the play area for the goals. Form two teams of three players each. Have each player choose an opposing player to guard.

Play begins with a jump ball between two opposing players in the middle of the play area. The team gaining possession of the ball starts on offense and advances the ball down the court by throwing and catching, and attempts to score (one point) by throwing the ball so that hits inside the opponent's mat. Offensive players with possession of the ball are able to run freely until tagged by a defensive player. At this point, the tagged player has to stop immediately and either pass or shoot the ball within five seconds. Defensive players cannot steal the ball out of the hands of an offensive player, but they can intercept or knock away a pass. Following each score, the non-scoring team takes immediate possession and begins play going in the opposite direction.

Touch Rugby

Introduction: This fun game is a simplified and non-contact modification of regular rugby. It develops throwing and catching skills—and requires a lot teamwork and hustle.

Number of Players: 6

Suggested Grade Levels: 4th–8th grades

Equipment: 1 rugby ball (or substitute a football), 4 cones

How to Play: Place two cones about 8-10 feet apart at each end of a rectangular-shaped play area for the goals. There are no boundary lines. Arrange the players into two equal teams of three players each. The teams start on their designated half of the play area. Designate one team to start with the ball on offense.

The object of the game is to score a touchdown by placing the ball on the floor past the opponent's goal. Play begins at midfield with one of the two offensive linemen throwing the ball backwards in an underhanded motion to the running back. The defensive team must start at least 5 yards away from the offensive linemen. The running back can run forward, or pass the ball backwards anytime to a teammate. The offensive player with possession of the ball can continue running forward toward the opponent's goal until tagged with two hands by a defensive player. This counts as a tackle and the play ends at that spot. If the ball is dropped or hits the ground at any time during play, the play is also over and counts as a down. After each play, the three offensive players line up in the same positions as before and play continues. The offensive team has up to six downs to score. If the offensive team does not score after the sixth down, the ball goes over to the other team at the spot of the last touch and they now have up to six downs to score going in the opposite direction.

Tug-o-War Doubles

Introduction: This traditional favorite is played by children around the world. It's a contest of strength, coordination, and teamwork.

Number of Players: 4

Suggested Grade Levels: 2nd–8th grades

Equipment: 1 tug-o-war rope, 2 cones

How to Play: Form two equal teams of two players each. Place the tug-o-war rope (about 12 feet in length) on the floor. Position a cone about two feet away on each side of the center mark. Both teams begin by stationing themselves on their side of the rope. Players will have more space and better balance by alternating sides of the rope when positioning for the contest.

On a signal, both teams start pulling. The contest ends when one of the teams pulls the center of the rope to their cone. Have the teams play several times with players in different positions each time.

As a safety precaution, remind the players to never let go of the rope. Also, players should quickly get back up on their feet if they fall.

Variation: Consider playing a version of tug-o-war that does not require a rope. The players clasp their hands around the waist of the player in front of them, and pull. This game always provides lots of fun!

Multi-Way Tug-o-War

Introduction: This is a challenging variation of the classic Tug-o-War contest.

Number of Players: 4–6

Suggested Grade Levels: 2nd–8th grades

Equipment: 1 four-way tug-o-war rope (or a rope tied into a circle), beanbags

How to Play: Have each player pick up the circular or four-way rope with one hand, stretching it tightly. The players should be facing outward. The instructor places a beanbag in front of each player on the ground so that it is just out of reach of the player's free hand.

On a signal, the players start pulling, trying to pick up their beanbag without letting go of the rope. The first player to pick up his or her beanbag is declared the winner. Play several times with players in different positions each time.

As a safety precaution, players should quickly get back up on their feet if they fall.

Index
(Alphabetical by Game)

About the Author

Guy Bailey, M.ED., has over 30 years of experience teaching physical education at the elementary and middle school levels. He currently teaches elementary physical education in the North Clackamas School District which is located in Milwaukie, Oregon. During this time, he has also directed many after-school sport activities and coached numerous youth sports. His educational background includes having a B.S. degree (Central Washington University) and a M.Ed. degree (Portland State University) in his specialty area of physical education.

In addition to this title, Guy has authored five other books in the area of physical education. *The Physical Educator's Big Book of Sport Lead-Up Games* (2003) is widely considered the most comprehensive resource of games used to develop sport skills ever published. His popular book, *Recess Success* (2007), is a special collection of more than 200 playground and recess games for the elementary school. It is a revised and updated version of *The Ultimate Playground & Recess Game Book,* a book he originally authored in 2001. *The Ultimate Homeschool Physical Education Game Book* (2004) is a unique resource aimed at helping home schooling families teach physical education skills in the home and backyard setting. In 2007, Guy authored *Gym Scooter Fun & Games*, the first book ever published on the subject of gym scooter games and activities.

As a physical educator, Guy's goal is to equip each of his students with a wide range of movement skills coupled with a love of movement. He believes that *lasting* skill learning in physical education needs to consist of success-oriented experiences that literally leave children craving for more. His books reflect this philosophy of using learning activities that are both skill based and fun.

Guy resides in Vancouver, Washington. He has four children—Justin, Austin, Carson, and Heather. Guy enjoys family time together, exercising, writing, hiking, and attending PAC-12 intercollegiate sporting events in the Pacific Northwest.

94699984R00130

Made in the USA
Middletown, DE
22 October 2018